NOT WHAT I SIGNED UP FOR STUDY GUIDE

NOT WHAT I SIGNED UP FOR

Nicole *Unice*

STUDY GUIDE

A SIX-WEEK SERIES

TYNDALE
MOMENTUM®

A Tyndale nonfiction imprint

Visit Tyndale online at tyndale.com.

Visit Tyndale Momentum online at tyndalemomentum.com.

Visit the author at nicoleunice.com.

Tyndale, Tyndale's quill logo, *Tyndale Momentum*, and the Tyndale Momentum logo are registered trademarks of Tyndale House Ministries. Tyndale Momentum is the nonfiction imprint of Tyndale House Publishers, Carol Stream, Illinois.

Not What I Signed Up For Study Guide: A Six-Week Series

Cover designed by Julie Chen

Published in association with Jenni Burke of Illuminate Literary Agency: www.illuminateliterary.com.

For information about special discounts for bulk purchases, please contact Tyndale House Publishers at csresponse@tyndale.com, or call 1-855-277-9400.

ISBN 978-1-4964-4870-5

Printed in the United States of America

30	29	28	27	26	25	24
7	6	5	4	3	2	1

Contents

First Things First: A Word to Readers *1*

SESSION 1: The Joseph Blessing *7*

SESSION 2: The Promises He Keeps *41*

SESSION 3: The Tests of Your Character *77*

SESSION 4: The Work of Patience *109*

SESSION 5: The Power of Redemption *141*

SESSION 6: The Story of Sovereignty *173*

A Note for Leaders *200*
Appendix: Promises of God *205*
Notes *209*
About the Author *211*

FIRST THINGS FIRST: A WORD TO READERS

Hello, friend, and welcome to the journey!

My guess is that you are here because you've found yourself in a season you never expected, feeling things you never thought you'd feel, and maybe even navigating the unsettling experience of questioning ideas and people you never doubted in the past.

Life can throw you off-kilter, whether that's happened because of an earthquake-sized demolition to your story or a few subtle cracks in your foundation that have slowly caused your outlook to shift. Even if you aren't currently in a "not what I signed up for" season, chances are good that you have been in one before—and that you might be in one again.

Over these six sessions, whether you gather with a group or work through this study on your own, I invite you to grow in your understanding of God's faithfulness even through your trials, know His love right in the middle of your suffering, and stand firm in trust even when things remain paralyzingly uncertain.

Though the characters and the plot of your unexpected season are unique, I offer a few suggestions that should be helpful as you prepare for the journey:

First, allow yourself (and if in a group, everyone else) permission to be in a confusing space. Rather than trying to explain your circumstances, fix them, or numb them away, you will discover that healing and growth start when you simply acknowledge where you are and look for God to meet you there.

Second, begin cultivating a deep compassion for your own soul. Entering into your story with the lens of redemption is an act of will, and it takes time, courage, and patience.

When I started running again after knee surgery, I would repeat a mantra to myself to the cadence of my feet: *Take it easy, take it light, take it slow.*

Easy, light, and slow is the pace of the healing, uprooting, and replanting that God can do within you right now. Soul work is slow work. You can move only at the pace of your soul, and if you push it to go fast, it will hide. You will begin to just go through the motions, showing up for your study or group or reading but not actually being present. As author Parker Palmer said,

> Like a wild animal, the soul is tough, resilient, resourceful, savvy, and self-sufficient. . . . If we want to see a wild animal, we know that the last thing we should do is go crashing through the woods yelling for it to come out. But if we will walk quietly into the woods, sit patiently at the base of a tree, breathe with the earth, and fade into our surroundings, the wild creature we seek might put in an appearance. We may see it only briefly and only out of the corner of an eye—but the sight is a gift we will always treasure as an end in itself.[1]

Over the course of our journey together, your soul is invited to show up and meet with God. My job is to help set up the conversation between you and the Lord by bringing you Scripture and questions that will allow you to find your story within God's great story. It's a chance for your soul to speak about what you have experienced, the cares you need to bring to God's throne of grace, and the wounds and losses that you need God to redeem. To facilitate this relationship, you'll find daily exercises. Some days allow more time for quiet listening, not just responding to questions. That may be uncomfortable if you prefer to have clear direction, but discomfort is sometimes what's needed to make enough space to be honest with yourself and God about where you are and what you need. I promise, though, always to give you prompts and words to help you along the way!

SESSION RHYTHMS

Each group session includes:

- **Weekly Reading**
- **Main Point**
- **Video Notes**
- **Opening Group Conversation**
- **To the Word Together**
- **Application**
- **A Closing Prayer**

Because I've found that the only way to experience God every day is to spend intentional time with Him, the individual study is broken up into five days for each week. This gives you time for your own practice with God and time in worship to round out your week. If you fall behind or get stuck on any homework, don't let it derail your progress. Our souls move at different speeds and require different amounts of input, so you may find that responding to just a question or two each day draws you close to God, while someone else may choose to complete every single prompt. Your journey is your journey, no matter how long it takes you to get to the end.

Finally, you can either work through this study on your own or ask a few friends to join you. You might even consider bringing this study to your church. God has designed us to live out our stories with other people. The psalmist David offers us this invitation: "Glorify the LORD with me; let us exalt his name together" (Psalm 34:3). Sometimes the only thing that sustains us in our own struggles is knowing that someone else has felt God's comfort or experienced God's love in their life that week. We can borrow another person's faith when our own feels weak. And if you are brave enough to lead a group (especially for the first time!), please check out the leader's guide in the back of this study.

To recap, here's a quick list of what you'll need to get started:

Group:

You can work through this content individually or in a group. A smaller group of five to eight people allows for good conversation time. Larger groups can view the video together and then break into smaller units for discussion. To increase vulnerability and build trust, it's best for the same groups to meet over the six sessions.

Materials:

Each participant will need a copy of the *Not What I Signed Up For* book and this study guide. You can also access the streaming video series, which contains my companion video teaching for each session, at rightnowmedia.org.

Readings:

Because this study guide is a companion to *Not What I Signed Up For*, each session corresponds to chapters in that book. At the start of each group session, you'll find a list of the chapters to read that week. You can do so at any time; however, you'll be prompted to read particular chapters on specific days. If you haven't already done so, that is the ideal time to read them.

Time:

Each session is structured to take between seventy-five and ninety minutes, including time for additional connection before or after the teaching. If you do this study over a lunch break or in a virtual group, you could save time by focusing on the study only. The personal studies are designed to take about twenty minutes each day.

Personal Study:

Each week includes five personal study days, with time spent both studying Scripture and reading assigned sections from *Not What I Signed Up For*. The group discussion each week will be based on this reflection time.

I am so encouraged that you are taking this journey. I don't know how you arrived here or what condition your soul is in, but what I do know is that the source of life—true life, abundant life, healed and redeemed life—is Jesus Christ. And when we bring ourselves to God, we will never be forsaken or forgotten. We are never failures, and we are never too far gone to know true relationship with Jesus, the very One who stretched out His arms in sacrifice on a cross. Your journey of restoration begins as soon as you open your heart to God's love and allow Him to shape the great story of your life.

THE JOSEPH BLESSING

Real and redeemed people are re-created people,
made in the image of God and moving toward the holiness of Christ.

NOT WHAT I SIGNED UP FOR, PAGE 12

What do we do when we don't know what to do?

All of us face times when life doesn't go as planned. In those seasons, our trust in God's goodness is tested. We need a resilient faith to not just survive these times but to come through them with a deeper relationship with God and a stronger love for people. The story of Joseph paints a compelling picture of a life centered in that kind of faith. Within the story, you'll discover how tests and trials can lead you toward forgiveness, redemption, and hope. This week, let's learn about Joseph's triumph—the ending of the story that will frame the rest of our study together.

⭐ MAIN POINT

Unexpected seasons are always an invitation to develop a deeper trust in God's love for you.

Tune in to video session 1: "The Joseph Blessing"

▶ VIDEO NOTES

1. Unexpected seasons demand a response.

2. God uses stories to give us a framework of understanding and response.

3. We have the gift of the beautiful ending through which we can interpret the rest of our stories.

👥 OPENING GROUP CONVERSATION

1. An unexpected season is a period of life with an unknown timeline and an unsure outcome. In dealing with uncertainty and waiting, we may respond in several ways. **Do you tend to: a. skip and stuff; b. dive and dwell; or c. swing between the two?**

2. God uses stories to give us a framework for meaning, and one of the most powerful ways we experience life is through narrative. **Name a few books or movies that you love. Are there any common themes in those stories?**

3. We have the benefit of knowing the end of Joseph's story, as poignantly captured in Joseph's words of redemption to his brothers:

Don't be afraid. Am I in the place of God? You intended to harm me, but God intended it for good to accomplish what is now being done, the saving of many lives.

GENESIS 50:19-20

Joseph makes this statement at the end of his ordeal when he can look back and clearly see God at work. It can be challenging to have this perspective when you're in the middle of a trying season. **When your circumstances are difficult, which of the following descriptions are most true of you? Circle all that apply, or adjust the statement(s) to be accurate for you.**

a. I find myself anxious about the future.

b. I second-guess my decisions and blame my past choices for this pain.

c. I often find myself blaming others or my circumstances for my pain.

d. I feel like I'm being punished.

e. I have a hard time trusting God's intentions, and I wonder if He has forgotten about me.

f. I feel angry about what's happened.

g. I feel resigned that nothing can change.

📖 TO THE WORD TOGETHER

Let's go to a few passages that illuminate how we tend to respond to God in uncertainty, as well as how He responds to us.

1. **Read aloud together the passage below.** Pay attention to Peter's response:

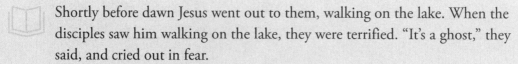

> Shortly before dawn Jesus went out to them, walking on the lake. When the disciples saw him walking on the lake, they were terrified. "It's a ghost," they said, and cried out in fear.
>
> But Jesus immediately said to them: "Take courage! It is I. Don't be afraid."
>
> "Lord, if it's you," Peter replied, "tell me to come to you on the water."
>
> "Come," he said.
>
> Then Peter got down out of the boat, walked on the water and came toward Jesus. But when he saw the wind, he was afraid and, beginning to sink, cried out, "Lord, save me!"
>
> Immediately Jesus reached out his hand and caught him. "You of little faith," he said, "why did you doubt?"
>
> And when they climbed into the boat, the wind died down.
>
> MATTHEW 14:25-32

a. How do the disciples respond when they first see Jesus' figure walking on the water?

b. What does Peter do after Jesus identifies Himself?

c. How does Jesus respond?

d. Why do you think this moment is so significant to the disciples?

2. **Now read this Old Testament passage together. Consider "Israel" and "Jacob" as synonyms for God's people and then reflect on how this passage's principles apply to us:**

"To whom will you compare me?
  Or who is my equal?" says the Holy One.
Lift up your eyes and look to the heavens:
  Who created all these?
He who brings out the starry host one by one
  and calls forth each of them by name.
Because of his great power and mighty strength,
  not one of them is missing.

Why do you complain, Jacob?
  Why do you say, Israel,
"My way is hidden from the LORD;
  my cause is disregarded by my God"?
Do you not know?
  Have you not heard?

The Lord is the everlasting God,
> the Creator of the ends of the earth.
He will not grow tired or weary,
> and his understanding no one can fathom.
He gives strength to the weary
> and increases the power of the weak.
Even youths grow tired and weary,
> and young men stumble and fall;
but those who hope in the Lord
> will renew their strength.
They will soar on wings like eagles;
> they will run and not grow weary,
> they will walk and not be faint.

ISAIAH 40:25-31

a. What proof of His power does God provide?

b. What are some of the promises He makes about Himself?

c. What promises does He make about His engagement with His people?

🔦 APPLICATION

Before we get into the details of Joseph's life, we begin at the ending: when Joseph's season of uncertainty and waiting is resolved and he is reconciled to his brothers. He reassures them, "Don't be afraid. Am I in the place of God? You intended to harm me, but God intended it for good to accomplish what is now being done, the saving of many lives" (Genesis 50:19-20).

We learn three important promises from Joseph's words of comfort as his brothers struggle to believe they are forgiven and restored:

1. Do not be afraid.
2. God is here.
3. God has plans to accomplish good for you and through you.

I want to invite you to bring to God an uncertain season or circumstance that comes to your mind. Allow yourself to feel the weight of your unanswered questions. Imagine yourself taking the whole story and laying it out in front of God's throne.

Now imagine God showing you a date on the celestial calendar when everything is resolved and you are completely full of joy and peace about that unexpected season.

1. What emotions present themselves when you imagine that?

2. If you knew without a shadow of a doubt that resolution was coming, how would you live differently tomorrow?

3. In Scripture, the word *heart* is best translated as the inner place where our thoughts, emotions, and beliefs intersect. **What beliefs or thoughts might be influencing your feelings around the situation you've been imagining?**

This is the heart of the matter—when we turn toward Christ in uncertainty, we experience the deepest growth in our faith.

YOUR ONE THING

As the group closes, take two minutes to record one key takeaway from this session.

What words or ideas do you want to hang on to as you go into this week?

A CLOSING PRAYER

God, give us faith to believe You're at work in our stories.

God, give us faith to believe Your intentions are good.

God, give us faith to believe . . . You.

ON YOUR OWN

DAILY STUDY

SESSION 1

THE HEART OF THE MATTER

 READ

Introduction and chapter 1, Not What I Signed Up For

Use this space to capture any key phrases or takeaways from the chapter that you want to remember:

No matter how long we've been following Jesus, there is one question we must continue to ask ourselves, especially as we face trials of all kinds. The question is, *What does being a person of faith mean to me?*

Seasons of life and the inevitable trials that come will force us to move—either toward a joy and peace beyond our circumstances or toward a more superficial, more anxious, and less secure life. The difficult thing about this choice is that it's *not* determined by the quantity of religious activity on our calendars but by the quality of interaction with Christ in our hearts. And unexpected seasons always test and refine the heart.

In today's passage, we read the resolution of Joseph's story in his own words. More than thirty years after his brothers sold the teenage Joseph into slavery, they are still fearful of his revenge. But Joseph has a different interpretation of his own suffering—based not on circumstances but on faith. The way he views his responsibility and God's sovereignty determines Joseph's clarity, peace, and ability to forgive.

Today we are going to address the heart of the matter when it comes to our own uncertain seasons—understanding the state of our faith.

REFLECT

In this week's video session and reading, we experience a living picture of what faith looked like for Joseph, found in this redemptive ending: "Don't be afraid. Am I in the place of God? *You intended to harm me, but God intended it for good to accomplish what is now being done, the saving of many lives* (Genesis 50:19-20, emphasis added).

1. As you consider times when you struggle to see God at work in your life or when you feel disconnected from Him, which of these three promises from the passage is the hardest for you to believe?

   a. Do not be afraid (be at peace).

   b. God is here (rest in God's sovereignty).

   c. God has plans to accomplish good for you and through you (experience blessing and purpose).

Take a few moments to write down any questions or objections that come to mind concerning that promise:

Uncertain seasons in our lives are always an invitation. We are encouraged to consider whether we may have accidentally relocated our faith from the certainty of our unseen God to the certainty of our known circumstances. When we are shaken, we will be disturbed! When we feel shaken in circumstances, it is natural that we also feel shaken in faith. But in this season, we have the chance to rightfully reposition our earthly circumstances and relationships so that the supremacy and sovereignty of God become our greatest source of joy.

This process moves us:

- from uncertainty to God's clarity
- from turmoil to peace
- from being troubled in spirit to having joy in Christ

And it always starts with the heart of the matter: faith. This week, let's start by defining what faith is and what it can be in our lives, and then move through each promise during our time with God.

2. Hebrews 11:1 offers us a definition of faith. **Review the verse in the following translations, underlining the words or phrases that stand out to you.**

Now faith is confidence in what we hope for and assurance about what we do not see.

NIV

Now faith is the assurance (title deed, confirmation) of things hoped for (divinely guaranteed), and the evidence of things not seen [the conviction of their reality—faith comprehends as fact what cannot be experienced by the physical senses].

AMP

Faith is the reality of what we hope for, the proof of what we don't see.

CEB

The fundamental fact of existence is that this trust in God, this faith, is the firm foundation under everything that makes life worth living. It's our handle on what we can't see.

MSG

   a. Record a definition of faith based on these translations:

CLOSING MEDITATION

It's so easy to believe that a blessed life means a life free of pain, strife, or suffering, but that is *not* how God defines blessing (more on that later in the study). **For now, let's look at what the Bible clearly says about what we should expect in our earthly lives:**

God is our refuge and strength,
    an ever-present help in trouble.
Therefore we will not fear, though the earth give way
    and the mountains fall into the heart of the sea,
though its waters roar and foam
    and the mountains quake with their surging.

PSALM 46:1-3

I know the LORD is always with me.
    I will not be shaken, for he is right beside me.

PSALM 16:8, NLT

As you close your time with God, reflect on what He says about Himself in these passages. Take a moment or two to consider God as "refuge," God as "strength," or God as "with me." **Jot down a prayer in which you tell Him what one (or all three!) of these promises means to you right now.**

To get you started writing out your prayers, here's an example from my own devotion time:

Father, You being my refuge means that I always have a safe place to go. When the world feels overwhelming or I feel like I'm going to be swallowed up by the emotions and struggles of today, I thank You that You always invite me to dwell with You in this safe and protected space of Your love.

DO NOT FEAR

In a 2022 survey of Americans, almost nine out of ten reported daily anxiety about inflation, with more than 60 percent reporting daily anxiety over everything from health to relationships to global events.[1]

Our recent history is full of trials that tempt us toward fear, whether it presents itself as a low rumble of worry in the background of our minds or a crippling anxiety that controls our every decision. When it comes to fear, the Bible has good news and bad news for us. First, the bad news: Fear is as present a reality today as it was when the Bible was written, and there is no promise that circumstances will improve in a way that would give us reason *not* to fear.

But the good news? What God promises is not deliverance from fearful circumstances but deliverance from fearful hearts. In Genesis 50, Joseph's first words for his brothers were *do not be afraid*. The good news Joseph gave to his brothers pales in comparison to the good news we find in Jesus, who repeatedly affirms that we do not need to be afraid. In Christ, we can live in uncertainty and still have peace.[2]

 REFLECT

1. Mark the following scales as your assessment of how much fear you experience in each area:

Finances

Not fearful — Daily concern

1 2 3 4 5 6 7 8 9 10

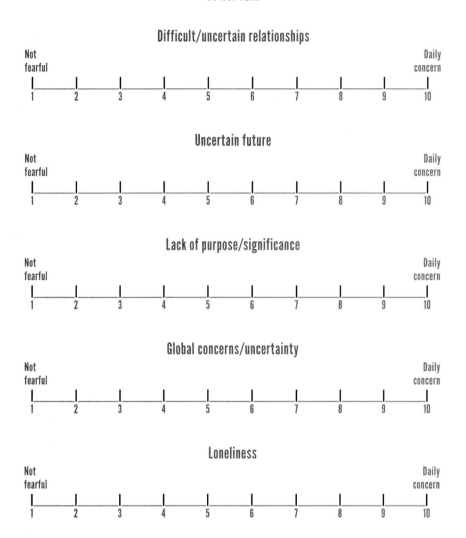

Difficult/uncertain relationships

Not
fearful

Daily
concern

1   2   3   4   5   6   7   8   9   10

Uncertain future

Not
fearful

Daily
concern

1   2   3   4   5   6   7   8   9   10

Lack of purpose/significance

Not
fearful

Daily
concern

1   2   3   4   5   6   7   8   9   10

Global concerns/uncertainty

Not
fearful

Daily
concern

1   2   3   4   5   6   7   8   9   10

Loneliness

Not
fearful

Daily
concern

1   2   3   4   5   6   7   8   9   10

If other categories or specifics come to mind, list them here:

2. Now, let's turn to God's Word together. Read the following passages:

"So be strong and courageous! Do not be afraid and do not panic before them. For the LORD your God will personally go ahead of you. He will neither fail you nor abandon you."

Then Moses called for Joshua, and as all Israel watched, he said to him, "Be strong and courageous! For you will lead these people into the land that the LORD swore to their ancestors he would give them. You are the one who will divide it among them as their grants of land. Do not be afraid or discouraged, for the LORD will personally go ahead of you. He will be with you; he will neither fail you nor abandon you."

DEUTERONOMY 31:6-8, NLT

Don't love money; be satisfied with what you have. For God has said,

"I will never fail you.
    I will never abandon you."

So we can say with confidence,

"The LORD is my helper,
    so I will have no fear.
    What can mere people do to me?"

Remember your leaders who taught you the word of God. Think of all the good that has come from their lives, and follow the example of their faith.

HEBREWS 13:5-7, NLT

a. Make a short list of the instructions given within these passages:

3. Now read Jesus' words below. Underline any word that appears at least twice:

> But when the Father sends the Advocate as my representative—that is, the Holy Spirit—he will teach you everything and will remind you of everything I have told you.
>
> I am leaving you with a gift—peace of mind and heart. And the peace I give is a gift the world cannot give. So don't be troubled or afraid.
>
> JOHN 14:26-27, NLT

Friends, I cannot stress enough how crucial it is that we understand the marvelous gifts that Jesus promises us. First, we need to know what those gifts are, and second, we must understand how we receive them.

a. What is the gift promised by Jesus in the John 14 passage?

b. On Pentecost, the apostle Peter was filled with the Spirit and shared the gospel with thousands of people who had never heard it. He told them, "Repent and be baptized, every one of you, in the name of Jesus Christ for the forgiveness of your sins. And you will receive the gift of the Holy Spirit" (Acts 2:38). What does this verse tell us about how we initially receive the primary gift Christ promised to send?

Our security comes from understanding and receiving the gifts promised to us by God through Christ. Choosing not to examine our gifts would be like leaving beautifully wrapped gifts under the Christmas tree because we were too busy to open them! Unfortunately, many believers live like this—intellectually acknowledging Christ as Lord but never actually experiencing the marvelous gifts of His presence. If that sounds like you, my prayer is that you would put your faith on the line, beginning with releasing your fears. Let this unexpected season draw you closer to God. Dare Him to show up in your life by helping you change the way you think, starting today.

 ## CLOSING MEDITATION

Look back over your list of concerns and place them before the Father today. Use the Scriptures you've read to shape a prayer. Write your own, or follow this rhythm:

Lord,

I confess my worries about _____ [be specific].

   I know You say in Your Word _____ [repeat His promises].

      I want to believe these promises for me today. I long to experience Your peace in my thoughts, feelings, and actions. Whenever anxiety rises up today, let me become more aware of Your presence. I thank You for this gift and receive it from You even now.

Spend a few moments breathing in deeply the peace of Christ. Let yourself focus on the idea of receiving this incredible gift and the feelings that being the recipient of God's great love brings.

GOD IS HERE

In our group work for week 1, we looked at a passage in which Jesus calls out to Peter through the storm. In today's passage, we encounter another storm—and an opportunity to understand the true source of peace even in the most fearful circumstances.

Below, read the story in Mark 4 and picture yourself in the scene.

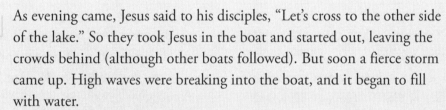

As evening came, Jesus said to his disciples, "Let's cross to the other side of the lake." So they took Jesus in the boat and started out, leaving the crowds behind (although other boats followed). But soon a fierce storm came up. High waves were breaking into the boat, and it began to fill with water.

Jesus was sleeping at the back of the boat with his head on a cushion. The disciples woke him up, shouting, "Teacher, don't you care that we're going to drown?"

When Jesus woke up, he rebuked the wind and said to the waves, "Silence! Be still!" Suddenly the wind stopped, and there was a great calm. Then he asked them, "Why are you afraid? Do you still have no faith?"

The disciples were absolutely terrified. "Who is this man?" they asked each other. "Even the wind and waves obey him!"

MARK 4:35-41, NLT

💡 REFLECT

1. In the passage above, two different experiences cause the disciples to fear. First, they are frightened by the storm. But once Jesus calms the wind and waves, "the disciples were absolutely terrified. 'Who is this man?' they asked each other.

'Even the wind and waves obey him!'" (verse 41, NLT). **According to this verse, what scared them?**

Fear is a part of the human experience. But there are different kinds of fear: the fear that comes from our own constructed assumptions about how life is supposed to be or what will make us happy, and a healthy fear, or reverence, of the One who controls all circumstances.

We'll be taking a deep dive into the story of Joseph during the upcoming sessions of this study, but this week we continue to focus on the end of the story. When Joseph looks back over his own experiences and suffering, his succinct reflection is: "Am I in the place of God?" (Genesis 50:19).

In other words, Joseph was able to trust in the power and sovereignty of God moving through his circumstances, even difficult ones. We don't often use *fear* this way in our vocabulary; but in the Bible, this kind of fear is like respect on turbo setting: It's the kind of respect for who God is that allows us to settle into our lives with security.

In today's story, we see that Christ has sovereignty, or power, over the wind and waves.

2. **Read the following passage from John's Gospel:**

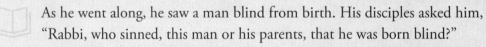

As he went along, he saw a man blind from birth. His disciples asked him, "Rabbi, who sinned, this man or his parents, that he was born blind?"

"Neither this man nor his parents sinned," said Jesus, "but this happened so that the works of God might be displayed in him. As long as it is day, we must do the works of him who sent me. Night is coming, when no one can work. While I am in the world, I am the light of the world."

After saying this, he spit on the ground, made some mud with the saliva, and put it on the man's eyes. "Go," he told him, "wash in the Pool of Siloam" (this word means "Sent"). So the man went and washed, and came home seeing.

JOHN 9:1-7

a. What does Christ have power over in this passage?

3. Read the passage below from the Gospel of Luke:

Soon afterward, Jesus went to a town called Nain, and his disciples and a large crowd went along with him. As he approached the town gate, a dead person was being carried out—the only son of his mother, and she was a widow. And a large crowd from the town was with her. When the Lord saw her, his heart went out to her and he said, "Don't cry."

Then he went up and touched the bier they were carrying him on, and the bearers stood still. He said, "Young man, I say to you, get up!" The dead man sat up and began to talk, and Jesus gave him back to his mother.

They were all filled with awe and praised God. "A great prophet has appeared among us," they said. "God has come to help his people." This news about Jesus spread throughout Judea and the surrounding country.

LUKE 7:11-17

a. What does Christ have power over in this passage?

 ## CLOSING MEDITATION

These passages show that Jesus Christ came to manifest both the power of God over the world and our circumstances and the love of God to meet us in the reality and difficulty of life. Faith is believing that God *does* have power over our circumstances, even if facing that reality makes us confused or angry about what He allows in our lives. But our faith grows only when we face that reality, making that truth our starting point in the pursuit of a deeper life of trust and peace in God.

With that in mind, take a few moments to confess what you need to hand over to God's control today. **You might want to journal a prayer following this prompt:**

Jesus, You control the wind and the waves, and You control _____ [name a challenging circumstance, relationship, or situation]. Jesus, You have power over sight and over life, so I confess Your power over _____. Give me faith to believe that even in these circumstances that I cannot control and do not like, You meet me with Your comfort and Your confidence.

Sustain me with Your loving hand today. I ask for Your help with _____. Amen.

GOD HAS PLANS

Trusting that God has plans for us is key to moving from uncertainty to clarity and from turmoil to peace. Nothing is more powerful than recognizing God's sovereignty—the truth that He *is* in control, even in the most difficult of circumstances. So many of us struggle with this truth because there is so much we *can't* understand and *don't know how* to reconcile, whether it be the wars in the world or the wars we've fought in our own lives. We grow in trust as we step into this gap, no matter how dark it seems, and ask God to show us His plans for good, even in the worst of our troubles.

We can begin by using God's Word to build a foundation that goes beyond our experience. Joseph's blessing to his brothers is one example. It reveals his understanding that even in the worst experience—one meant for evil—God had intentions for good. In the midst of a difficult season, it may feel hard to believe that God has good plans, but His Word, His actions, and the sacrifice of His Son all point to a God of love who will redeem and restore.

To begin today's study, read Ephesians 1:3-14. It's a dense passage, so take it slowly. As you read, underline the verbs—the action words. For example, in the first two verses, you'll see *blessed*, *loved*, and *chose*. These are all actions God takes toward His people.

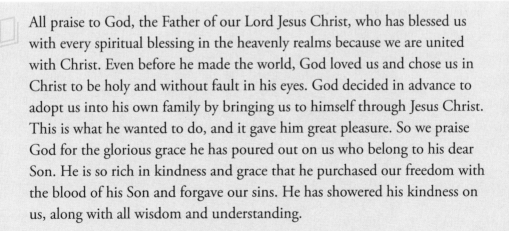

All praise to God, the Father of our Lord Jesus Christ, who has blessed us with every spiritual blessing in the heavenly realms because we are united with Christ. Even before he made the world, God loved us and chose us in Christ to be holy and without fault in his eyes. God decided in advance to adopt us into his own family by bringing us to himself through Jesus Christ. This is what he wanted to do, and it gave him great pleasure. So we praise God for the glorious grace he has poured out on us who belong to his dear Son. He is so rich in kindness and grace that he purchased our freedom with the blood of his Son and forgave our sins. He has showered his kindness on us, along with all wisdom and understanding.

God has now revealed to us his mysterious will regarding Christ—which is to fulfill his own good plan. And this is the plan: At the right time he will bring everything together under the authority of Christ—everything in heaven and on earth. Furthermore, because we are united with Christ, we have received an inheritance from God, for he chose us in advance, and he makes everything work out according to his plan.

God's purpose was that we Jews who were the first to trust in Christ would bring praise and glory to God. And now you Gentiles have also heard the truth, the Good News that God saves you. And when you believed in Christ, he identified you as his own by giving you the Holy Spirit, whom he promised long ago. The Spirit is God's guarantee that he will give us the inheritance he promised and that he has purchased us to be his own people. He did this so we would praise and glorify him.

EPHESIANS 1:3-14, NLT

 ## REFLECT

1. Read the Ephesians 1 passage again, paying special attention to the verbs you've underlined. In the columns below, record each action God takes and each action we take.

ACTIONS GOD TAKES	ACTIONS WE TAKE

2. These lists reveal God's great plan for us. Verse 12 explains the purpose of this plan: "God's purpose was that we Jews who were the first to trust in Christ would bring praise and glory to God" (NLT). **Put this plan in your own words:**

3. In the English Standard Version, verse 12 ends with the phrase "to the praise of his glory." I've provided a few definitions to help with this tricky but important phrase:

   Praise is "an expression of approval."[3]
   Glory is "greatness," "splendor," an "external manifestation of his [God's] being."[4]

   When you consider those definitions, how would you use your own words to describe God's life plan for you as for "the praise of his glory"?

Friend, we could never out-dream God's dreams for us. His great pleasure is to see us shine brightly with the light of His presence—and His presence is beautiful, righteous, loving, and good. He has plans for all of us—and they always maximize the reflection of His glory in our lives.

God has plans. God has plans for *you*.

 ## CLOSING MEDITATION

As we close our time, I want to invite you to do one of two optional meditations:

1. If reading Ephesians 1 fills you up—if you know this truth in your heart—spend a few moments offering God praise for the way you've seen Paul's words play out in your life.

2. If you wrestle to believe that Ephesians 1 could be true for you, take a moment to write God's Word into your heart. Record this passage below, but as if it's written directly to you and about you. Every time the pronoun "us" appears, write your name instead. Pay attention to the thoughts and emotions that come to mind, and then bring them before God. Ask Him to help you believe that His love and plans for you are real and powerful.

GOD INTENDS GOOD

 READ

Chapter 2, Not What I Signed Up For

Use this space to capture any key phrases or takeaways from the chapter that you want to remember:

We've spent our first week slowly exploring the Joseph blessing, a living picture of what we can experience regardless of our uncertainty or trouble:

- Do not be afraid.
- God is here.
- God has plans to accomplish good for you and through you.

Can you imagine living each day as if you believed this blessing to be true for you, in every season, regardless of any uncertainty or trouble that comes? As we'll discover together in our study of Joseph's story, believing these promises is a hard-won victory. It requires grit: persevering through the tests, growing in deeper trust, and allowing God to write our victory stories in His way, for His glory.

 ## REFLECT

I've chosen a couple of passages that speak of the goodness of God—and the good plans He has for us.

Psalm 116 gives us a glimpse of what it looks like to be both honest *and* trusting. **Read through the psalm, bringing to mind any uncertainty you are facing right now and singing this song back to God.**

Underline the phrases you resonate with. Circle the phrases you want to believe for yourself.

I love the LORD because he hears my voice
    and my prayer for mercy.
Because he bends down to listen,
    I will pray as long as I have breath!
Death wrapped its ropes around me;
    the terrors of the grave overtook me.
    I saw only trouble and sorrow.
Then I called on the name of the LORD:
    "Please, LORD, save me!"

How kind the LORD is! How good he is!
    So merciful, this God of ours!
The LORD protects those of childlike faith;
    I was facing death, and he saved me.
Let my soul be at rest again,
    for the LORD has been good to me.
He has saved me from death,
    my eyes from tears,
    my feet from stumbling.
And so I walk in the LORD's presence
    as I live here on earth!
I believed in you, so I said,
    "I am deeply troubled, LORD."
In my anxiety I cried out to you,
    "These people are all liars!"
What can I offer the LORD
    for all he has done for me?
I will lift up the cup of salvation
    and praise the LORD's name for saving me.
I will keep my promises to the LORD
    in the presence of all his people.

The LORD cares deeply
    when his loved ones die.
O LORD, I am your servant;
    yes, I am your servant, born into your
        household;
    you have freed me from my chains.
I will offer you a sacrifice of thanksgiving
    and call on the name of the LORD.
I will fulfill my vows to the LORD
    in the presence of all his people—

in the house of the LORD
in the heart of Jerusalem.

Praise the LORD!

PSALM 116, NLT

You may notice that the psalmist talks about two actions that sound foreign to our ears: lifting up the cup of salvation and offering a sacrifice of thanksgiving. In the book of Leviticus, we learn about the different sacrifices God required of His people. (Offering sacrifices is no longer required because of the work of Christ, but understanding the sacrifices is helpful as we consider how we engage with God each day.)

Unlike a sacrifice offered because of wrongdoing, a thank offering was given to celebrate the relationship between God and the person making the sacrifice. The cup of salvation was lifted up as a sign of victory and a celebration of the deliverance and forgiveness offered by God to His people.

We know that salvation is what we receive when we believe in Christ—His divinity, His death and resurrection, and His living presence in our lives—but salvation is also an ongoing process of living into the ways we've been saved by God, over and over again: saved from our sin, saved from our guilt, saved from our anxiety, saved from our turmoil, saved from our doubt.

 ## CLOSING MEDITATION

Be gentle with yourself as we close this time. Imagine your heavenly Father smiling and receiving you with open arms. What do you need to be saved from today? Ask Him and thank Him for what He's already done and what He continues to do in your life. **You may want to use some of the language from Psalm 116 to write your own prayer here:**

As we dive into the story of Joseph together in the coming weeks, my prayer for you is the one Paul wrote to the church in Thessalonica:

> So we keep on praying for you, asking our God to enable you to live a life worthy of his call. May he give you the power to accomplish all the good things your faith prompts you to do. Then the name of our Lord Jesus will be honored because of the way you live, and you will be honored along with him. This is all made possible because of the grace of our God and Lord, Jesus Christ.
>
> **2 THESSALONIANS 1:11-12, NLT**

This is the blessing of our life in Christ—as we live not for ourselves but for Him. Not glorifying ourselves but glorifying Him. Not praising ourselves but praising Him for the gifts He gives us, forgiving us again and again and again.

THE PROMISES HE KEEPS

God does not play hide-and-seek when it comes to these
tests. He uses this time to reveal to us what is in our hearts:
who we are becoming and what we are believing.

NOT WHAT I SIGNED UP FOR, PAGE 64

Unexpected seasons start with loss. That loss might be the deep pain of grief or betrayal, or the inevitable losses we face whenever change comes into our lives. Loss often destabilizes us and invites us to consider the question, *How solid is my foundation?* This week we'll explore how we find our footing again—even if we've fallen into a pit.

 MAIN POINT

A foundation of faith will not fail even when all else does.

 RECAP

Look over last week's homework. **Share any of your reflections from what you learned during your daily studies or while reading the first few chapters of *Not What I Signed Up For.***

Tune in to video session 2: "The Promises He Keeps"

 VIDEO NOTES

1. Family dysfunction isn't a modern phenomenon; it's a real consequence of sin that shows up in living color in Genesis.

2. We know God by faith, but we pass on blessing through faith and deed.

3. The test of loss is always an invitation to communion.

OPENING GROUP CONVERSATION

In today's lesson, we explored Joseph's (very) dysfunctional family. As we enter into the story of Joseph's abandonment by his brothers, we are invited to consider how our own families have shaped the way we engage with unexpected seasons now.

1. As a kid, were you ever lost or left behind? Share your story with the group. What emotions did you experience back then? What did that situation teach you about life?

2. What's one lesson or family value from your childhood that you have maintained as an adult? What's one lesson or value you've decided to leave behind?

TO THE WORD TOGETHER

Last week in our homework we started with the question we all must answer: *What does being a person of faith mean to me?* As we continue to explore that question in our individual study over the coming weeks, we'll read a few Scripture passages together.

Let's look at a few places that give us a sense of what it means to live with a faith that won't fail.

1. Read aloud the following passage from the Gospel of Mark.

A large crowd followed and pressed around him. And a woman was there who had been subject to bleeding for twelve years. She had suffered a great deal under the care of many doctors and had spent all she had, yet instead of getting better she grew worse. When she heard about Jesus, she came up behind him in the crowd and touched his cloak, because she thought, "If I just touch his clothes, I will be healed." Immediately her bleeding stopped and she felt in her body that she was freed from her suffering.

At once Jesus realized that power had gone out from him. He turned around in the crowd and asked, "Who touched my clothes?"

"You see the people crowding against you," his disciples answered, "and yet you can ask, 'Who touched me?'"

But Jesus kept looking around to see who had done it. Then the woman, knowing what had happened to her, came and fell at his feet and, trembling with fear, told him the whole truth. He said to her, "Daughter, your faith has healed you. Go in peace and be freed from your suffering."

MARK 5:24-34

a. Summarize the story in your own words.

b. What do we learn about faith based on the woman's inner dialogue?

2. Now let's read a story that occurs just slightly after the story of the healed woman:

Jesus left there and went to his hometown, accompanied by his disciples. When the Sabbath came, he began to teach in the synagogue, and many who heard him were amazed.

"Where did this man get these things?" they asked. "What's this wisdom that has been given him? What are these remarkable miracles he is performing? Isn't this the carpenter? Isn't this Mary's son and the brother of James, Joseph, Judas and Simon? Aren't his sisters here with us?" And they took offense at him.

Jesus said to them, "A prophet is not without honor except in his own town, among his relatives and in his own home." He could not do any miracles there, except lay his hands on a few sick people and heal them. He was amazed at their lack of faith.

MARK 6:1-6

a. Summarize the story in your own words.

b. What do we learn about faith based on the people's dialogue?

3. Let's compare the passages:

   a. What are some similarities between the bleeding woman and the crowd in Jesus' hometown? What are some differences?

   b. As you compare and contrast these two encounters with Jesus, what do you learn about faith?

What we begin to see in these passages is a principle that can be impactful to our own experience with God:

Faith requires belief, and our faith can grow and shrink. Growth in our faith comes from putting our belief into practice.

4. This week in our personal study, we will explore how our faith can become active even through tests of loss and integrity. Here's one clear promise of Scripture that can inform our conversation around faith.

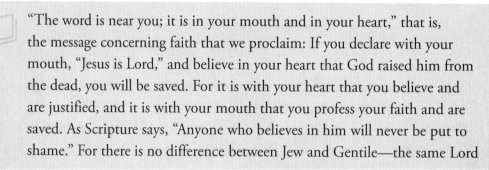

"The word is near you; it is in your mouth and in your heart," that is, the message concerning faith that we proclaim: If you declare with your mouth, "Jesus is Lord," and believe in your heart that God raised him from the dead, you will be saved. For it is with your heart that you believe and are justified, and it is with your mouth that you profess your faith and are saved. As Scripture says, "Anyone who believes in him will never be put to shame." For there is no difference between Jew and Gentile—the same Lord is Lord of all and richly blesses all who call on him, for, "Everyone who calls on the name of the Lord will be saved."

How, then, can they call on the one they have not believed in? And how can they believe in the one of whom they have not heard? And how can they hear without someone preaching to them? And how can anyone preach unless they are sent? As it is written: "How beautiful are the feet of those who bring good news!"

But not all the Israelites accepted the good news. For Isaiah says, "Lord, who has believed our message?" Consequently, faith comes from hearing the message, and the message is heard through the word about Christ.

ROMANS 10:8-17

a. According to this passage, what is the message of faith?

b. How do we receive faith?

What good news God has given us through Christ! Our faith is not the result of our deeds or misdeeds. It is not given because we were born into the right family or achieved some kind of status on heaven's rankings of good deeds. Faith is the result of believing. It is the foundation from which we can interpret and understand even the most difficult of seasons.

APPLICATION

The passages from Mark on pages 44–45 invite us to examine the ways we might draw near or withdraw from Jesus.

1. In what past circumstances have you reached out to grasp on to Jesus? In what type of situations have you noticed that people are most open to reaching out for help? How is that true in your own life?

2. In what ways might we be like the people in Jesus' hometown who "took offense" at Jesus (Mark 6:3)? In what circumstances have you wanted to oppose God?

This week in our homework we'll explore two gifts that often present themselves through the tests of loss and tests of integrity. The first gift is communion—a deep sense of God's presence, acceptance, and mercy. The second gift is clarity—the knowledge of what is worth fighting for.

As a group, take a few moments to reflect quietly on the gifts of communion and clarity. Write down any questions, objections, or requests that come to mind when you think about those words:

YOUR ONE THING

As the group closes, take two minutes to record one key takeaway from this session.

What words or ideas do you want to hang on to as you go into this week?

A CLOSING PRAYER

God, give us faith to believe You're at work in our stories.
God, give us faith to believe Your intentions are good.
God, give us faith to believe . . . You.

We ask for the joy that comes from Your presence,
the confidence that comes from Your acceptance,
the healing that comes with Your mercy,

and the great blessing of Your love. Amen.

ON YOUR OWN
DAILY STUDY

SESSION 2

BLESSING, DEFINED

If we want to get the world's hot take on blessings, we need look no further than a hashtag or search engine. The hashtag #blessing has been used almost 150 million times on Instagram. A Google search on blessing returns queries on such wide-ranging topics as incantations, elves, video games, and pop songs. Clearly, we are interested in being blessed but understandably confused about exactly what blessing is and who is eligible to receive it. Friend, this is one area in which we do not have to be confused. It is not just our responsibility to understand this concept but our right to claim true blessing as sons and daughters of God.

It's time to sharpen your pencils, because we are going to take a deeper dive into Scripture today. The only way to come to God's Word is with faith. **Take a moment to pray:**

Father, only You can illuminate Your words for me so I can understand them. Shine light into my heart and clarity into my mind as I learn about Your love for me through Your Word. Amen.

Today, let's take a look at what the Bible teaches us about blessing and how that provides us direction for how we can interpret our own trials.

First, a definition:

bless
1. To hallow or consecrate
2. To invoke divine care for
3. To praise, glorify
4. To speak well of: approve

5. To protect, preserve
6. To endow, favor[1]

As you read through the passage below from Genesis 15, pay attention to the various ways we might use the word *blessing*. Keep in mind that Joseph was a descendent of Abram and would likely have been very familiar with the following story and what it meant to be blessed by God.

After this, the word of the LORD came to Abram in a vision:

"Do not be afraid, Abram.
   I am your shield,
      your very great reward."

But Abram said, "Sovereign LORD, what can you give me since I remain childless and the one who will inherit my estate is Eliezer of Damascus?" And Abram said, "You have given me no children; so a servant in my household will be my heir."
   Then the word of the LORD came to him: "This man will not be your heir, but a son who is your own flesh and blood will be your heir." He took him outside and said, "Look up at the sky and count the stars—if indeed you can count them." Then he said to him, "So shall your offspring be."
   Abram believed the LORD, and he credited it to him as righteousness.

GENESIS 15:1-6

Abram was promised a son—even though he and his wife had never been able to have children and were growing old (Abram would be one hundred and his wife ninety years old when their son was to be born). Although all was stacked against them, although Abram had no earthly reason to believe, he believed God anyway. He took Him at His word.
   Abram (who would later have his name changed by God to Abraham) became the father of Isaac, who became the father of Jacob. Abraham, Isaac, and Jacob are the

first of God's chosen people, who become known as the Israelites (or Hebrews, and eventually Jews). They are *blessed* by God to be a blessing to the world—to show all of God's creation what it looks like to be in relationship with Him.

Fast-forward through all of the Israelites' story in the Old Testament to the coming of Jesus, God in the flesh. He came to make known that the blessings of God's chosen people were not limited to one race or people group, but that His blessing extends to all. **Let's connect the passage we read in Genesis to a very important point in the New Testament book of Romans.**

REFLECT

1. Underline the word *righteousness* every time it appears in the passage:

What does Scripture say? "Abraham believed God, and it was credited to him as righteousness."

Now to the one who works, wages are not credited as a gift but as an obligation. However, to the one who does not work but trusts God who justifies the ungodly, their faith is credited as righteousness. David says the same thing when he speaks of the blessedness of the one to whom God credits righteousness apart from works:

"Blessed are those
   whose transgressions are forgiven,
   whose sins are covered.
Blessed is the one
   whose sin the Lord will never count against them." . . .

Against all hope, Abraham in hope believed and so became the father of many nations, just as it had been said to him, "So shall your offspring be." Without weakening in his faith, he faced the fact that his body was as good as dead—since he was about a hundred years old—and that Sarah's womb was also dead. Yet he did not waver through unbelief regarding the promise of God, but was strengthened in his faith and gave glory to God, being fully persuaded that God had power to do what he had promised. This is why "it was credited to him as righteousness." The words "it was credited to him" were written not for him alone, but also for us, to whom God will credit righteousness—for us who believe in him who raised Jesus our Lord from the dead. He was delivered over to death for our sins and was raised to life for our justification.

ROMANS 4:3-8, 18-25

2. What caused Abram to be credited with righteousness?

3. According to verse 20, Abraham "did not waver through unbelief regarding the promise of God, but was strengthened in his faith and gave glory to God." What does this tell us about the result of this righteousness?

4. Who is credited with righteousness today?

This is the blessing! This is the fruit of our belief and the heart of our faith. Blessing is ultimately about our relationship with God and about how we display His splendor through the transformation of our lives. God's glory is known because of the blessings He gives—not material wealth, not earthly comfort, not even your own health—but because of the way He meets our most important needs.

5. Now that we know that the blessing of Abraham is also our blessing, read the following passage and underline everything God promises to do for Israel (and so will also do for you). I've done the first one for you:

"Remember these things, Jacob,
    for you, Israel, are my servant.
I have made you, you are my servant;
    Israel, I will not forget you.
I have swept away your offenses like a cloud,
    your sins like the morning mist.
Return to me,
    for I have redeemed you."

Sing for joy, you heavens, for the LORD has
        done this;
    shout aloud, you earth beneath.
Burst into song, you mountains,
    you forests and all your trees,
for the LORD has redeemed Jacob,
    he displays his glory in Israel.

ISAIAH 44:21-23

God promises that He has not forgotten His people, that He sweeps away their offenses, and that He redeems them. These are the promises of blessing!

6. What does the last line of this passage say God receives as a result of the blessing He pours out?

 ## CLOSING MEDITATION

As you close your time with God today, use the Scriptures we've studied to write your own definitions of blessing and righteousness as a prayer.

Dear God, my blessing comes because You _____. God, You've made me righteous because _____. Lord, thank You that I am Your chosen one and that You display Your glory in my life. Today, whether I go through happy times or hard times, through mourning or dancing, may You get the glory. Amen.

LOSS

 READ

Chapter 3, *Not What I Signed Up For*

Use this space to capture any key phrases or takeaways from the chapter that you want to remember:

Often, unexpected seasons in our lives begin with a loss. Whether that loss is something that we choose, like the loss of comfort when leaving home for the first time, or whether it comes in a way we never would have chosen, loss is as constant in life as change. So when we engage with questions of our faith, we have to engage with any emotions that impact our outlook—and loss will always create emotion, whether we acknowledge it or not! Today we enter into the opening scenes in Joseph's life, which begin with a great emptying—a loss of comfort, security, relationship, and safety.

As you read through the chapter, ask God to open your heart to any emotions that come up, and allow any memories that might surface to enter into God's healing presence. It doesn't matter whether those memories are recent or ancient, whether they are unresolved or even make you uncomfortable. Simply bring them into your awareness and allow them to be a part of this journey.

REFLECT

Psychology has identified four types of grief that aren't connected to death:[2]

- **Loss of identity**—This comes when a role or connection that we had a strong emotional attachment to fails to continue. For instance, a retiree may experience the loss of significance and importance she felt for thirty years in her role as an elementary school teacher.
- **Loss of safety**—This happens when a physical, relational, sexual, or spiritual boundary is manipulated or violated. For instance, an experience of sexual abuse can make the whole world feel unsafe; a traumatic loss of relationships in church may lead someone to question their faith.
- **Loss of autonomy**—This is the inability to live and manage independently, either because someone depends on you or you must depend on another. For instance, you may lose independence when you become a parent for the first time or have a child with special needs. If you develop an illness or face a life situation that requires you to give up your own independence, you may also lose a sense of autonomy.
- **Loss of dreams**—Perhaps the most painful and misunderstood of all, the loss of dreams leads to the confusion and pain from something—whether it's one's career, friendships, or relationship status—not working out as planned.

These losses are as significant as death to us, because in many ways, they are a death. We lose someone or something we love, even if that something is the dream we were holding on to about our own preferred future. With loss always comes grief—and it doesn't go away quietly.

NOT WHAT I SIGNED UP FOR, PAGES 37–38

1. Using the descriptions on page 60, name the three to five losses (including any significant losses from death) that come to mind when you think through your own story:

This is a key area where we might be tempted to either skip and stuff or dive and dwell, so it's important to reflect on how losses have shaped our faith (for better or worse).

2. When you think through your own experiences with loss, how would you characterize your relationship with God in the midst of it? Check any/all that apply.

☐ I don't know what to do with my sadness, so I skip it and stuff it.

☐ I feel angry and confused about why some things have happened and tend to dwell on it.

☐ I've tried to process these losses, but I feel stuck.

☐ I realize that God has been close to me and that my faith has grown through loss.

☐ Other:_____.

CLOSING MEDITATION

It's very likely that different losses have impacted your faith differently. But the test of loss is an invitation to communion, as we'll talk about tomorrow. **For today, let's close with a promise from Scripture that always stands, no matter how dark our circumstances:**

> But this I call to mind,
>   and therefore I have hope:
> The steadfast love of the LORD never ceases;
>   his mercies never come to an end;
> they are new every morning;
>   great is your faithfulness.
> "The LORD is my portion," says my soul,
>   "therefore I will hope in him."
>
> **LAMENTATIONS 3:21-24, ESV**

COMMUNION

Today you'll begin taking a closer look at Joseph's story. Although the details may feel very removed from your life today, there is still an overwhelmingly human tone to Joseph's experience of betrayal, jealousy, emptying, and weeping. God uses these circumstances—the searing pain within dysfunctional families, missed opportunities, and wounds given and received—to invite us to enter into the story.

Let's start by reading Genesis 37. Some of the key verses are below.

Jacob loved Joseph more than any of his other children because Joseph had been born to him in his old age. So one day Jacob had a special gift made for Joseph—a beautiful robe. But his brothers hated Joseph because their father loved him more than the rest of them. They couldn't say a kind word to him.

GENESIS 37:3-4, NLT

Joseph's brothers went to pasture their father's flocks at Shechem. When they had been gone for some time, Jacob said to Joseph, "Your brothers are pasturing the sheep at Shechem. Get ready, and I will send you to them."

"I'm ready to go," Joseph replied. . . .

When Joseph's brothers saw him coming, they recognized him in the distance. As he approached, they made plans to kill him. "Here comes the dreamer!" they said. "Come on, let's kill him and throw him into one of these cisterns. We can tell our father, 'A wild animal has eaten him.' Then we'll see what becomes of his dreams!"

GENESIS 37:12-13, 18-20, NLT

Judah said to his brothers, "What will we gain by killing our brother? We'd have to cover up the crime. Instead of hurting him, let's sell him to those Ishmaelite traders. After all, he is our brother—our own flesh and blood!" And his brothers agreed. So when the Ishmaelites, who were Midianite traders, came by, Joseph's brothers pulled him out of the cistern and sold him to them for twenty pieces of silver. And the traders took him to Egypt. . . .

Then the brothers killed a young goat and dipped Joseph's robe in its blood. They sent the beautiful robe to their father with this message: "Look at what we found. Doesn't this robe belong to your son?"

Their father recognized it immediately. "Yes," he said, "it is my son's robe. A wild animal must have eaten him. Joseph has clearly been torn to pieces!" Then Jacob tore his clothes and dressed himself in burlap. He mourned deeply for his son for a long time. His family all tried to comfort him, but he refused to be comforted. "I will go to my grave mourning for my son," he would say, and then he would weep.

Meanwhile, the Midianite traders arrived in Egypt, where they sold Joseph to Potiphar, an officer of Pharaoh, the king of Egypt. Potiphar was captain of the palace guard.

GENESIS 37:26-28, 31-36, NLT

 REFLECT

1. As you read Genesis 37:1-36, list all the losses you notice Joseph, Jacob, and Joseph's brothers sustaining:

Genesis 37 captures a comprehensive emptying—everything Joseph held on to for meaning and purpose was stripped away. Although this chapter is silent on God's response to his suffering, Joseph's future actions point to his faith in God's provision, protection, and presence in his life.

Joseph was empty, but his heart was still full.

Fast-forward along the arc of history and consider when Jesus came into the world. He entered quietly and humbly. The book of Isaiah prophesied that Jesus would have "no beauty or majesty to attract us to him" (53:2). After about thirty years of anonymity, Jesus began to teach. When the apostle Matthew recorded what is considered the greatest sermon ever preached, he began with these words from Jesus:

> Blessed are the poor in spirit,
>   for theirs is the kingdom of heaven.
> Blessed are those who mourn,
>   for they will be comforted.
>
> MATTHEW 5:3-4

The Message translation expresses verse 4 this way: "You're blessed when you feel you've lost what is most dear to you. Only then can you be embraced by the One most dear to you." The Bible consistently connects the pain of suffering with the gift of God's comfort and presence.

2. Reread Matthew 5:3-4 and list what Jesus says those who are blessed will receive:

A hard but beautiful truth about our lives is this: It is often in our greatest losses that we become empty enough of ourselves and our own comfort to be able to be filled by Christ.

3. **Read the following passages. Underline all the gifts that suffering or trials can bring to our lives. I've done the first one for you.**

Dear friends, don't be surprised at the fiery trials you are going through, as if something strange were happening to you. Instead, be very glad—for <u>these trials make you partners with Christ in his suffering</u>, so that you will have the wonderful joy of seeing his glory when it is revealed to all the world.

1 PETER 4:12-13, NLT

We are confident that as you share in our sufferings, you will also share in the comfort God gives us.

2 CORINTHIANS 1:7, NLT

Through suffering, our bodies continue to share in the death of Jesus so that the life of Jesus may also be seen in our bodies.

2 CORINTHIANS 4:10, NLT

Since he himself has gone through suffering and testing, he is able to help us when we are being tested.

HEBREWS 2:18, NLT

It was good for me to be afflicted
    so that I might learn your decrees.
The law from your mouth is more precious to me
    than thousands of pieces of silver and gold.

PSALM 119:71-72

Your losses cannot be rushed through, but at the same time, staying angry at or distant from God only makes your pain worse. As you're working through pain, you can be angry or frustrated with God, but the worst kind of pain is trying to get through suffering without Him near.

Drawing close to God—even when you have questions—involves committing your life to Him. It's placing your hope in the promises of God even when you can't find the strength to stand. It's claiming what you can know even in all that you don't know.

Here is a promise that matters:

> Come close to God, and God will come close to you. Wash your hands, you sinners; purify your hearts, for your loyalty is divided between God and the world.
>
> **JAMES 4:8, NLT**

Your losses often magnify how little the world can actually deliver. And they are an opportunity to place your loyalty squarely back with God, to wash your hands and purify your heart of anything you are harboring or holding back from God's healing touch and loving presence.

Dear friend, as I write these words for you, my heart aches for the loss and suffering you are feeling. I know you are tormented by the what-could-have-beens. You are replaying the scenarios and feeling the swirl of sadness, regret, anger, or shame—or maybe all of those at the same time. Although you can't change the past or rush the process of grief, you can rest in the present. You can cast your cares on Jesus, who knows what it is like to suffer. You can draw near to Him in your pain because He experienced every human pain. Even if you don't feel His presence, He is right there beside you.

4. Today we are going to begin the practice of simply resting in God's presence. **Try one of the exercises below as you seek to enter into God's rest.** We'll return to this practice throughout our study.

   a. Listen to worship music and let the words speak for you. Here are a few options that might resonate:

   "Nothing Else"—Cody Carnes

   "Never Have to Be Alone"—CeCe Winans

   "I Will Wait for You (Psalm 130)"—Shane and Shane

b. Meditate on one promise of God to center your heart and release your anxiety. You can repeat one phrase from Scripture, perhaps from a verse on the previous pages. Or you might simply say, "Jesus, my life is Yours," or "God, I receive Your love."

c. Journal or draw the promises of God, however that looks for you.

If simply being with God is difficult to practice, start with five minutes, and return to it. The mercy of God is abundant and powerful. His presence is healing and comforting. Communion with God is always available to you, whether you are in the deepest pit or darkest prison. God is with you. God sees you. God loves you.

 ## CLOSING MEDITATION

Let's close with the promises of God that are true for all of us today:

> Yes, my soul, find rest in God;
>   my hope comes from him.
> Truly he is my rock and my salvation;
>   he is my fortress, I will not be shaken.
> My salvation and my honor depend on God;
>   he is my mighty rock, my refuge.
> Trust in him at all times, you people;
>   pour out your hearts to him,
>   for God is our refuge.
>
> **PSALM 62:5-8**

INTEGRITY

 READ

Chapter 4, Not What I Signed Up For

Use this space to capture any key phrases or takeaways from the chapter that you want to remember:

The test of integrity naturally follows the test of loss. Integrity is always about matters at the rock bottom of who we are, examined when things we love are stripped away. We enter deeply into our own reality when we face unexpected seasons. We have to confront the truth of who we really are, what we really care about, how we are really doing. All of this "reality" can be difficult to manage, but the test of integrity is also an invitation to discover clarity, which comes when our comfortable identity feels stripped away, and what we value most and who we really are surface.

NOT WHAT I SIGNED UP FOR, PAGE 54

💡 REFLECT

As you consider the tests of integrity that you face in your unexpected season, consider this invitation: "We have to confront the truth of who we really are, what we really care about, how we are really doing." The prompts below will help you recognize what drives you.

1. **Unexpected seasons reveal what is shaping your identity.** List any lies you are tempted to believe about yourself in times of loss or tests of character:

2. **Unexpected seasons uncover what you value most.** List any values that you've realized are deeply important to you:

3. **Unexpected seasons test your resilience.** What three feeling words would you use to describe where you are today?

If you'd like some help in making your lists, see the small sample of options below. You may relate to something on this list or write your own:

LIES WE BELIEVE	VALUES WE HOLD	FEELINGS WE FEEL
"I am not enough."	Honesty	Angry
"I'm too needy."	Authenticity	Hopeful
"It's all my fault."	Loyalty	Joyful
"No one really understands me."	Success	Sad
"I'm a bad person."	Courage	Frustrated
"I'm forgotten."	Belonging	Fearful
"I've been abandoned."	Dependability/Faithfulness	Disgusted
"I can't trust anyone."	Diligence	Ambivalent
"I can't change."	Wisdom	Surprised
"I'm a failure."	Beauty	Trusting
"I'm unworthy of love."	Justice	Content

This kind of self-reflection can be difficult, but it is also a necessary part of moving toward freedom. When you are unmasked before God, you are your true self, even if that true self is discouraged, despairing, or confused. Note the benefits we gain from being willing to acknowledge what is driving us—good or bad.

If we walk in the light, as he is in the light, we have fellowship with one another, and the blood of Jesus, his Son, purifies us from all sin.
1 JOHN 1:7

Bring your true self before God without editing or trying to find a solution to your problems. Simply acknowledge where you are and who you are, and rest in the light of His healing presence.

CLOSING MEDITATION

Close your time by repeating or trying another idea from yesterday's homework.

Today we'll see what happens when Joseph's integrity is tested. Tests of integrity are moments of decision that clarify the strength of our willpower and the depth of our convictions.

Our own struggles (even when we fail!) can also clarify and realign our hearts around what really matters to us. This is the gift of testing from God.

The Hebrew word for *test* used in this verse from 1 Chronicles is *bahan*:

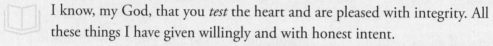

I know, my God, that you *test* the heart and are pleased with integrity. All these things I have given willingly and with honest intent.

1 CHRONICLES 29:17, EMPHASIS MINE

Read the following definition:

bahan: to try, prove, test, examine, search out. . . . The term is used primarily in a spiritual sense, and denotes an investigation to determine the essential character of a person, especially integrity.[3]

Notice that the fruit of integrity is not perfection; it's *honest intent.* Integrity is about our undivided hearts desiring what God desires. It's about knowing what He values and seeking after that in our daily lives. It does *not* mean we will stop messing up, struggling, or even suffering. Let's look closer at Joseph's test of integrity—and the painful consequences of his righteous choice. After all, Joseph soared through this integrity test in the spiritual sense, but I don't think landing in the king's prison felt like a victory in the earthly sense. Although he soared in God's eyes, he crashed and burned in everyone else's eyes.

Turn to Genesis 39 for today's reading.

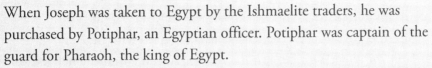

When Joseph was taken to Egypt by the Ishmaelite traders, he was purchased by Potiphar, an Egyptian officer. Potiphar was captain of the guard for Pharaoh, the king of Egypt.

The LORD was with Joseph, so he succeeded in everything he did as he served in the home of his Egyptian master. Potiphar noticed this and realized that the LORD was with Joseph, giving him success in everything he did. This pleased Potiphar, so he soon made Joseph his personal attendant. He put him in charge of his entire household and everything he owned. From the day Joseph was put in charge of his master's household and property, the LORD began to bless Potiphar's household for Joseph's sake. All his household affairs ran smoothly, and his crops and livestock flourished. So Potiphar gave Joseph complete administrative responsibility over everything he owned. With Joseph there, he didn't worry about a thing—except what kind of food to eat!

Joseph was a very handsome and well-built young man, and Potiphar's wife soon began to look at him lustfully. "Come and sleep with me," she demanded.

But Joseph refused. "Look," he told her, "my master trusts me with everything in his entire household. No one here has more authority than I do. He has held back nothing from me except you, because you are his wife. How could I do such a wicked thing? It would be a great sin against God."

She kept putting pressure on Joseph day after day, but he refused to sleep with her, and he kept out of her way as much as possible. One day, however, no one else was around when he went in to do his work. She came and grabbed him by his cloak, demanding, "Come on, sleep with me!" Joseph tore himself away, but he left his cloak in her hand as he ran from the house.

When she saw that she was holding his cloak and he had fled, she called out to her servants. Soon all the men came running. "Look!" she said. "My husband has brought this Hebrew slave here to make fools of us! He came into my room to rape me, but I screamed. When he heard me scream, he ran outside and got away, but he left his cloak behind with me."

She kept the cloak with her until her husband came home. Then she told him her story. "That Hebrew slave you've brought into our house tried to come in and fool around with me," she said. "But when I screamed, he ran outside, leaving his cloak with me!"

Potiphar was furious when he heard his wife's story about how Joseph had treated her. So he took Joseph and threw him into the prison where the king's prisoners were held, and there he remained. But the LORD was with Joseph in the prison and showed him his faithful love. And the LORD made Joseph a favorite with the prison warden. Before long, the warden put Joseph in charge of all the other prisoners and over everything that happened in the prison. The warden had no more worries, because Joseph took care of everything. The LORD was with him and caused everything he did to succeed.

GENESIS 39:1-23, NLT

 ## REFLECT

1. Genesis 39 repeatedly uses the phrase "the Lord was with Joseph." **What happened for Joseph because the Lord was with him?**

verse 3

verse 5

verse 21

verse 23

2. What was Joseph's reasoning for refusing Potiphar's wife?

3. How would you contrast Joseph's character with that of Potiphar's wife? Use three words to describe Joseph and three to describe her:

Reread the following from *Not What I Signed Up For*, chapter 4:

Despite the temptation he must have felt, Joseph understood that there is no such thing as a harmless sin. Despite pressure day after day, he resisted and then fled the temptation posed by one determined and unhappy woman. How does a person have the strength to make the hard choice? It comes from a vision for life that goes beyond the moment of testing. Joseph may have lost his family identity, his community, his language, his culture, and his place to worship; but what he still had was a dream, and he still had his stories. What he carried with him is the one thing you can also carry—specifically, the integrity that is rooted in the story of God's love in your life, the faith of those who have gone before you. Even in the worst unexpected season, if you still have integrity, you still have everything. And sometimes it's only in the pain of loss that we can discover with clarity what truly matters to us: the source of our integrity, the values we hold, the person we want to become. It doesn't happen quickly. It usually comes after several failed attempts. But the test of integrity brings a gift: an invitation to clarity.

PAGE 68

4. How would you define integrity in your own life?

5. Where is your integrity likely to be tested (e.g., relationships, inner thoughts/
   motivations, decisions, money, gossip, etc.)?

6. Have you ever suffered for doing the right thing? Imagine meeting with Jesus to
   talk about the times when your obedience has led to more pain in your life. What
   would you imagine Him saying to you?

 ## CLOSING MEDITATION

Let's close our time by resting in God's presence. **Consider confessing your own sin
and failings and recommitting to God's way in your life.**

*Praise God that "as far as the east is from the west, so far has he
removed our transgressions from us"! (Psalm 103:12). Praise God that
He is "the Father of compassion"! (2 Corinthians 1:3). Praise God that
"we are being renewed day by day" (2 Corinthians 4:16). Praise You,
Father, that You are never done loving us, guiding us, and shaping us
to become more like Your Son, Jesus Christ. Amen!*

THE TESTS OF YOUR CHARACTER

But Joseph did have to make choices in prison, and even if you are experiencing the limits of your season—perhaps even with all your rights and opportunities stripped away—you still have choices to make. You alone determine your attitude, your outlook, your hope.

NOT WHAT I SIGNED UP FOR, PAGE 76

Joseph's story is as dramatic as any blockbuster movie or novel. Just when we expect the good guy to prevail—he doesn't. The letdown is real when Joseph maintains his integrity with Potiphar's wife but is punished anyway. What do we do when doing the right thing doesn't yield our expected result? This week we'll journey together through the unexpected joy we can find in humility and the challenge of trusting God even as we wait.

⭐ MAIN POINT

Trusting God in our unexpected seasons is the rigorous journey to embedding a vital belief deep within us: God is powerful, and He is also good.

🗓 RECAP

Look over last week's homework. **Share any of your reflections from what you learned during your daily studies or how you practiced resting in God's presence.**

Tune in to video session 3: "The Tests of Your Character"

 **VIDEO NOTES**

1. The test of integrity is always an invitation to clarity.

2. Humility is a mix of presence and confidence; it makes us willing to help but also enables us to ask for help.

3. The test of humility is an invitation to joy.

4. Trusting God means holding together the tension of two true but often opposing things: God is powerful, and He is also good.

OPENING GROUP CONVERSATION

1. The teaching today opens with a closer look at humility. **How would you describe your relationship with humility? Circle all that apply.**

   a. I struggle with humility when it comes to not overcontrolling my life and relationships.

   b. I struggle with humility when it comes to admitting I need help.

   c. I struggle with humility when it comes to respecting and caring about people even after they've hurt me or someone I love.

   d. Other: _____.

2. Humility can be a difficult characteristic to describe, particularly because most of us have a blind spot about our own humility (or lack thereof). **Share about a person you've known whom you would describe as humble. Describe their overall disposition, their attitude toward themselves, and their engagement with others:**

3. Have you been through a season that required a deeper trust in God than ever before? Share with the group what that season was like and how it impacted your relationship with God.

📖 TO THE WORD TOGETHER

Let's work together to write a biblical definition of humility, describing what it means and how it plays out in our lives.

1. **Look up and read the following passages out loud together:**

   Psalm 25:9   Matthew 23:12
   Proverbs 11:2   Ephesians 4:2
   Proverbs 22:4   Philippians 2:3-8

   If you'd like, you can also use a concordance in your study Bible to look up *humble* and *humility* and see what other passages you find.

   a. **Now take a few minutes to write your own reflections on what humility means and how it applies to your life:**

2. **Next, read the passage below from Deuteronomy 8, looking for the reasons God tests or disciplines His people. Jot them in the space below the passage.**

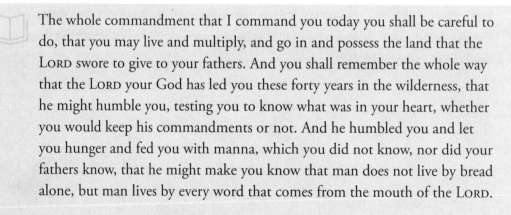

The whole commandment that I command you today you shall be careful to do, that you may live and multiply, and go in and possess the land that the LORD swore to give to your fathers. And you shall remember the whole way that the LORD your God has led you these forty years in the wilderness, that he might humble you, testing you to know what was in your heart, whether you would keep his commandments or not. And he humbled you and let you hunger and fed you with manna, which you did not know, nor did your fathers know, that he might make you know that man does not live by bread alone, but man lives by every word that comes from the mouth of the LORD.

Your clothing did not wear out on you and your foot did not swell these forty years. Know then in your heart that, as a man disciplines his son, the LORD your God disciplines you. So you shall keep the commandments of the LORD your God by walking in his ways and by fearing him. . . .

Take care lest you forget the LORD your God by not keeping his commandments and his rules and his statutes, which I command you today, lest, when you have eaten and are full and have built good houses and live in them, and when your herds and flocks multiply and your silver and gold is multiplied and all that you have is multiplied, then your heart be lifted up, and you forget the LORD your God, who brought you out of the land of Egypt, out of the house of slavery, who led you through the great and terrifying wilderness, with its fiery serpents and scorpions and thirsty ground where there was no water, who brought you water out of the flinty rock, who fed you in the wilderness with manna that your fathers did not know, that he might humble you and test you, to do you good in the end.

DEUTERONOMY 8:1-6, 11-16, ESV

 **APPLICATION**

1. Over the last two weeks, we've talked about various tests in life that present themselves: the test of loss, the test of integrity, the test of humility. **Which of those do you resonate with most? What do you think God is teaching you through that experience?**

Read aloud the following quotes from St. Alphonsus Liguori, an eighteenth-century Italian bishop: "He who trusts in himself is lost. He who trusts in God can do all things." He also said, "What does it cost us to say, 'My God help me! Have mercy on me!' Is there anything easier than this? And this little will suffice to save us if we be diligent in doing it."

To put it another way, when our faith is being tested, we are faced with this question: What could be easier than asking God to help us and have mercy on us? Yet so often, that is our last response.

2. **When you think about inviting God more deeply into your everyday life, what obstacles do you face? Circle all that apply.**

   a. I just don't think to do it.

   b. My problems seem too small for God to be concerned with.

   c. I've tried before, and I don't feel anything.

   d. My pride gets in the way, so I always seem to want to do everything myself.

   e. I'm too busy and stressed to remember one more thing.

   f. Other:_____.

What's one area of your life in which you'd like to trust God more deeply this week? Make a plan with your group for how you want to remember to invite God into the situation and ask for His mercy and help. You might set aside time in the morning, write out your prayers, set a reminder on your phone, or start a shared text with the group to encourage one another this week.

It is often in discovering God's love and mercy for us in the sustained, consistent, small ways each day that we begin to trust Him more deeply for the bigger questions and the harder seasons. Dear friends, let's spur one another on this week in the area that God has invited us to open up to Him so we can release our concerns into His loving care.

YOUR ONE THING

As the group closes, take two minutes to record one key takeaway from this session.

What words or ideas do you want to hang on to as you go into this week?

A CLOSING PRAYER

God, give us faith to believe You're at work in our stories.
God, give us faith to believe Your intentions are good.
God, give us faith to believe . . . You.

We ask for the joy that comes from Your presence,
the confidence that comes from Your acceptance,
the healing that comes with Your mercy,

and the great blessing of Your love.

Grant us the humility to serve others like You do
and the trust to believe that Your mercy covers our weaknesses
and that Your powerful grace overcomes our failings. Amen.

ON YOUR OWN
DAILY STUDY
SESSION 3

HOW TO DO THE RIGHT THING (EVEN WHEN IT HURTS)

One of the most remarkable parts of Joseph's story is the consistency with which he continued to do the right thing, even when it cost him. This week we enter into another dark season in Joseph's life. After being imprisoned for making the right decision and refusing Potiphar's wife, he now has another choice to make: Will he continue to show up with integrity and humility, or will the prison and the waiting get the best of him? And with Joseph as a model for the seasons in our own lives that feel confining and long, how do we persevere in always doing the next right thing?

The secret, friends, is not in trying harder, gripping more tightly, or shaming ourselves into better behavior. Our true place of love and righteousness isn't going to materialize in the same habits and patterns we already live within. The kind of integrity and righteousness that can stand up against the forces of this world comes only when we've been transformed from the inside out.

Today we are going to refresh ourselves by reading one of the most powerful Scripture passages about what happens when we are transformed by Christ. **As you read, underline every command (an imperative; for instance, the passage opens with the directive "Don't copy the behavior and customs of this world").**

Don't copy the behavior and customs of this world, but let God transform you into a new person by changing the way you think. Then you will learn to know God's will for you, which is good and pleasing and perfect. . . .

Don't just pretend to love others. Really love them. Hate what is wrong. Hold tightly to what is good. Love each other with genuine affection, and take delight in honoring each other. Never be lazy, but work hard and serve the Lord enthusiastically. Rejoice in our confident hope. Be patient in trouble, and keep on praying. When God's people are in need, be ready to help them. Always be eager to practice hospitality.

Bless those who persecute you. Don't curse them; pray that God will bless them. Be happy with those who are happy, and weep with those who weep. Live in harmony with each other. Don't be too proud to enjoy the company of ordinary people. And don't think you know it all!

Never pay back evil with more evil. Do things in such a way that everyone can see you are honorable. Do all that you can to live in peace with everyone.

Dear friends, never take revenge. Leave that to the righteous anger of God. For the Scriptures say,

> "I will take revenge;
>   I will pay them back,"
>   says the LORD.

Instead,

> "If your enemies are hungry, feed them.
>   If they are thirsty, give them something to drink.
> In doing this, you will heap
>   burning coals of shame on their heads."

Don't let evil conquer you, but conquer evil by doing good.

ROMANS 12:2, 9-21, NLT

REFLECT

1. Now look over your underlined phrases and choose the three to five that resonate most with you as areas in which you want to grow. Copy them here:

2. Review your notes on the definition of humility from the group study this week. Which verse or verses stand out to you most? Copy them here:

James 4:10 says, "Humble yourselves before the Lord, and he will lift you up in honor." (NLT). One of the fastest ways to humble yourself is to honestly assess the places where you've fallen short of God's commands. You and I don't do this to feel bad about ourselves—we do it to feel honest about ourselves. When we are honest about our failings, we are positioned to be so grateful for God's grace.

3. This week, we are going to practice humility every day through our prayers. Here's a simple framework to follow:

God, I praise you for _____.
God, I confess I fall short in _____.
God, I ask you to help me _____.

Your prayers don't have to be long, but they do need to be specific. Here are some examples from my own life:

God, I praise you for <u>the promise that you never fail me</u>. (See the appendix on page 205 for a list of the promises of God.)
God, I confess I've fallen short in <u>trusting you with my kids' futures, so I'm worried and anxious</u>.
God, I ask you to help me <u>trust you with what I can't control and help me to be a source of patience and joy to those around me</u>.

CLOSING MEDITATION

God, I praise you for _____.

God, I confess I've fallen short in _____.

God, I ask you to help me _____.

HUMILITY, CONTINUED

 READ

Chapter 5, *Not What I Signed Up For*

Use this space to capture any key phrases or takeaways from the chapter that you want to remember:

Thomas Merton wrote, "Pride makes us artificial, and humility makes us real."[1] Yesterday we began the practice of making ourselves "real" before God in both our honest assessment of our sin and our honest longings for help. Today let's continue engaging with these practices as we jump back into Joseph's story.

💡 REFLECT

Humility is a choice. It's allowing God to be the author and director of your story, even if that story is unfolding in the hospital room you hate or the workplace you dread or the pit or prison of your life—whatever that pit or prison looks like for you.

NOT WHAT I SIGNED UP FOR, PAGES 75–76

1. When you reflect on a difficult season in your life (perhaps one you're facing right now), in what way(s) does your relationship with God feel challenged? Circle all that apply.

   a. I don't know why God is allowing bad things to happen to me.
   b. I feel abandoned or alone.
   c. I don't know if God is punishing me or teaching me a lesson.
   d. Other: _____.

One great thing about unexpected seasons is they reveal false beliefs about ourselves or God that we might be holding on to. It's only when we let those misconceptions come into the light that we can release what's untrue and hold tightly to the promises God gives us.

2. Turn to the "Promises of God" list in the back of this study guide on page 205 (or use your own concordance). What promises do you need to remember in order to walk in the truth today? Write them down here:

After you've exposed the false beliefs that may be causing you to doubt God's presence, love, or faithfulness, you can turn to what *is* true and see that there can be good even in the most difficult season:

> Humility is seeing each day as an opportunity to gain knowledge, for "with the humble is wisdom."[2] Humility led Joseph to continue showing up to serve, to go above and beyond with anything he was given to do. . . . Even if you are experiencing the limits of your season—perhaps even with all your rights and opportunities stripped away—you still have choices to make. You alone determine your attitude, your outlook, your hope.
>
> *NOT WHAT I SIGNED UP FOR*, PAGE 76

3. If humility means "seeing each day as an opportunity to gain knowledge," what opportunities to grow would you say God is presenting to you right now?

You are the only one who can set your attitude for the day. **As you close this time, take the promises from Scripture that you recorded today and turn them into a prayer. For instance, if you want to adjust your attitude, you might pray from Ephesians 4:**

*God, thank You for considering me worthy of a calling!
I ask You to give me the strength and hope to see how
important I am in Your story and to take every
opportunity You give me today to love others as
You love them.
Amen.*

 **CLOSING MEDITATION**

Write your prayer here. Remember, it doesn't have to be perfect, it doesn't have to be long, and it doesn't even have to make sense to anyone but you! When you write out promises from Scripture, you are simply calling on God's faithfulness in a way that can transform your attitude.

HUMILITY, OBSERVED

Friend, I want to remind you that we are always works in progress. If we've been around Bible studies for a while, it can be easy to lull ourselves into spiritual laziness—talking the talk but not actually walking the walk! Our hearts easily deceive us (Jeremiah 17:9) and so moving toward the middle way—the real and redeemed way—takes work. On the one hand, we can slide into complacency; on the other, we can become legalistic or discouraged by all the ways we are not enough.

Neither of these approaches represents God's heart and His grace for us. The real and redeemed way allows the Holy Spirit to counsel us—to show us where we are growing while also revealing new ways we are called deeper into Christlikeness in our daily lives.

Some time later, Pharaoh's chief cup-bearer and chief baker offended their royal master. Pharaoh became angry with these two officials, and he put them in the prison where Joseph was, in the palace of the captain of the guard. They remained in prison for quite some time, and the captain of the guard assigned them to Joseph, who looked after them.

While they were in prison, Pharaoh's cup-bearer and baker each had a dream one night, and each dream had its own meaning. When Joseph saw them the next morning, he noticed that they both looked upset. "Why do you look so worried today?" he asked them.

And they replied, "We both had dreams last night, but no one can tell us what they mean."

"Interpreting dreams is God's business," Joseph replied. "Go ahead and tell me your dreams."

So the chief cup-bearer told Joseph his dream first. "In my dream," he said, "I saw a grapevine in front of me. The vine had three branches that began to bud and blossom, and soon it produced clusters of ripe grapes. I was holding Pharaoh's wine cup in my hand, so I took a cluster of grapes and squeezed the juice into the cup. Then I placed the cup in Pharaoh's hand."

"This is what the dream means," Joseph said. "The three branches represent three days. Within three days Pharaoh will lift you up and restore you to your position as his chief cup-bearer. And please remember me and do me a favor when things go well for you. Mention me to Pharaoh, so he might let me out of this place. For I was kidnapped from my homeland, the land of the Hebrews, and now I'm here in prison, but I did nothing to deserve it."

When the chief baker saw that Joseph had given the first dream such a positive interpretation, he said to Joseph, "I had a dream, too. In my dream there were three baskets of white pastries stacked on my head. The top basket contained all kinds of pastries for Pharaoh, but the birds came and ate them from the basket on my head."

"This is what the dream means," Joseph told him. "The three baskets also represent three days. Three days from now Pharaoh will lift you up and impale your body on a pole. Then birds will come and peck away at your flesh."

Pharaoh's birthday came three days later, and he prepared a banquet for all his officials and staff. He summoned his chief cup-bearer and chief baker to join the other officials. He then restored the chief cup-bearer to his former position, so he could again hand Pharaoh his cup. But Pharaoh impaled the chief baker, just as Joseph had predicted when he interpreted his dream. Pharaoh's chief cup-bearer, however, forgot all about Joseph, never giving him another thought.

GENESIS 40:1-23, NLT

REFLECT

1. What do you notice about Joseph's actions in the story? What clues does that give you about his character?

In this chapter, we see Joseph:

- remaining present and humble enough to notice the dejected spirits of the king's servants and then wanting to help;
- expressing his faith in God to people who would not know or believe in the same God;
- sharing his story and asking for help; and
- passing (another) integrity test when he chose to be honest about the meaning of the baker's dream.

2. Now look to your own life and follow this model as a way to evaluate your humility. On a scale of 1 to 7 (1 being "not at all like me" and 7 being "very much like me"), rate yourself in each of these areas:

   a. *I am present and attentive to the needs of those around me. I ask God to give me eyes to see how I can encourage and serve others each day.*

Not at all like me — Very much like me

1   2   3   4   5   6   7

b. *I am courageous with my testimony. When people ask me about the hope that I have, I share boldly about Jesus.*

c. *I am willing to be vulnerable about my own needs. I readily and often ask for help in the form of spiritual counsel and prayer. I avoid always being the "strong one" for others.*

d. *I choose honesty even when it comes at a cost. I endeavor to be clear and direct in the way I engage with others.*

3. In which of these areas would you say you have seen the most progress in your faith in your last (or current) hard season?

4. In which of these areas do you think God is continuing to invite you to grow?

Do not allow these scales to tip you toward shame or self-condemnation! Instead, allow them to be a mirror that helps you see more clearly how God is actively and intentionally calling you to grow in humility and love for others.

CLOSING MEDITATION

While the cupbearer forgot all about Joseph once he was restored to his position, God never forgot Joseph—and He will never forget you. Even better, He will never stop showering His mercy and love on you. **As you close, read this passage as a reminder of how God regards you. Underline everything God has done for you.**

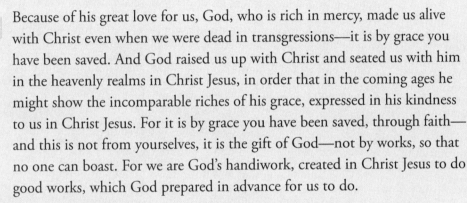

> Because of his great love for us, God, who is rich in mercy, made us alive with Christ even when we were dead in transgressions—it is by grace you have been saved. And God raised us up with Christ and seated us with him in the heavenly realms in Christ Jesus, in order that in the coming ages he might show the incomparable riches of his grace, expressed in his kindness to us in Christ Jesus. For it is by grace you have been saved, through faith—and this is not from yourselves, it is the gift of God—not by works, so that no one can boast. For we are God's handiwork, created in Christ Jesus to do good works, which God prepared in advance for us to do.
>
> EPHESIANS 2:4-10

Fill in the blanks to summarize how God regards you.

Because of His _____ _____, God regards me as His _____!

What a promise that brings confidence and hope for your day. Walk out in that truth as God calls you to express humility and love.

READ

Chapter 6, *Not What I Signed Up For*

Use this space to capture any key phrases or takeaways from the chapter that you want to remember:

Today we turn our attention to another theme that plays out in Joseph's story: trust, particularly in the form of waiting. We've defined our "not what I signed up for" season as a time with an unsure outcome and an unknown timeline. Too often we assume that, like a fallow field, nothing is happening when we feel stuck in our circumstances. Yet this is precisely the time when God can expand our hearts if we cultivate an attitude of thanksgiving. As John Ortberg wrote, "Gratitude is the ability to experience life as a gift. It opens us up to wonder, delight, and humility. It makes our hearts generous. It liberates us from the prison of self-preoccupation."[3] Let's take a closer look at what God does in the waiting.

💡 REFLECT

> Waiting is a fierce but fruitful teacher. In the rocky ground between what I hoped for and what I experienced is an opportunity for something entirely new to grow. I do not welcome this rocky ground, and frankly, I don't think I'm very good at cultivating it. But it seems as if some lessons can only be learned here.
>
> *NOT WHAT I SIGNED UP FOR*, PAGE 97

1. Have you experienced waiting as a "fierce but fruitful teacher"? What lessons have you learned in the waiting seasons of your life?

During our struggles, we can come to know God more deeply. One way we find God is through His acts of common grace, the small but beautiful ways He shows His presence in the world.

> When you are in a season in which nothing in your story seems good, focusing on the goodness you experience as His common grace can be your lifeline from one day to the next.
>
> *NOT WHAT I SIGNED UP FOR*, PAGE 102

2. Your assignment for today is to find ten common grace markers to celebrate. For instance, as I write this, I've become aware of several beautiful gifts: the warmth of the sun across my hands as I write, the beautiful diversity of the people in the

room where I'm working, and the smell of the freshly brewed coffee that fills my favorite ceramic mug.

 ## CLOSING MEDITATION

The "Something Good" list: Today, record as many things as possible that you appreciate. Aim to jot down at least ten—but hopefully many more!

1.

2.

3.

4.

5.

6.

7.

8.

9.

10.

More:

ANTINOMY

We close our week with one big and important concept for us to grasp as we wrestle with who God is when life is difficult. As we discovered in chapter 6 of *Not What I Signed Up For*, an antinomy is when two truths appear to contradict.

Why is this so important for us? Our minds want to close loops and do not like contradictions. We like when life is black and white. This can get us into all kinds of trouble, though, when it comes to everyday life. We want to find reasons, especially for bad things. We want to be able to blame ourselves, others, or spiritual forces outside of our control. If we are honest with ourselves, we want to blame God. We want to find a reason for our trouble so we can understand it. This is why antinomy matters—when we can embrace it, we embrace faith. Though we recognize that some things are beyond our understanding, we also believe we can trust the God who understands, has a purpose, and is holding it all together.

 ## REFLECT

The writer of Proverbs understood what it looks like to hold on to our faith in the midst of uncertainty:

 Trust in the LORD with all your heart and lean not on your own understanding; in all your ways submit to him, and he will make your paths straight.
PROVERBS 3:5-6

1. In order to trust in the Lord, what must we do?

2. In order to experience His straight paths, what must we do?

Notice the exclusive language used in this passage. God isn't looking for some of your heart or a few of your ways—He's commanding you to fully surrender every aspect of your understanding and action.

3. Now read the following passage from 1 Corinthians 1. Circle the words *foolish* and *foolishness* every time they appear.

For the message of the cross is foolishness to those who are perishing, but to us who are being saved it is the power of God. For it is written:

"I will destroy the wisdom of the wise;
   the intelligence of the intelligent I will frustrate."

Where is the wise person? Where is the teacher of the law? Where is the philosopher of this age? Has not God made foolish the wisdom of the world? For since in the wisdom of God the world through its wisdom did not know him, God was pleased through the foolishness of what was preached to save those who believe. Jews demand signs and Greeks look for wisdom, but we preach Christ crucified: a stumbling block to Jews and foolishness to Gentiles, but to those whom God has called, both Jews and Greeks, Christ the power of God and the wisdom of God. For the foolishness of God is wiser than human wisdom, and the weakness of God is stronger than human strength.

1 CORINTHIANS 1:18-25

For the Corinthians, the idea that the Cross was "foolishness" would feel very true. They would have found it impolite even to mention execution by crucifixion.[4] The idea that a holy and perfect God would allow Himself to be beaten, scorned, and shamed on behalf of other people just made no sense to the earthly system they knew—and it is still perplexing today. On its own, our human intelligence can't grasp why a God with the power to conquer would choose sacrifice and death instead. To believe in His plan of redemption demands faith.

Likewise, to believe that God has good purposes for even the worst suffering also requires faith. It starts with acknowledging that God knows things we don't and has purposes for everything. **Read from Isaiah:**

"For my thoughts are not your thoughts,
     neither are your ways my ways,"
          declares the LORD.
"As the heavens are higher than the earth,
     so are my ways higher than your ways
     and my thoughts than your thoughts.
As the rain and the snow
     come down from heaven,
and do not return to it
     without watering the earth
and making it bud and flourish,
     so that it yields seed for the sower and bread for the eater,
so is my word that goes out from my mouth:
     It will not return to me empty,
but will accomplish what I desire
     and achieve the purpose for which I sent it."

ISAIAH 55:8-11

4. God uses a law of creation (the water cycle!) to explain a law of His character. **What does He promise will always be true?**

Now read the rest of this passage.

> "You will go out in joy
>   and be led forth in peace;
> the mountains and hills
>   will burst into song before you,
> and all the trees of the field
>   will clap their hands.
> Instead of the thornbush will grow the juniper,
>   and instead of briers the myrtle will grow.
> This will be for the LORD's renown,
>   for an everlasting sign,
>   that will endure forever."
>
> **ISAIAH 55:12-13**

5. We live in the tension of not fully understanding why hardships happen but being comforted by promises that enable us to have trust and joy. **According to verses 12-13, what does God promise will happen in the end?**

When it comes to trusting God, we need knowledge—but knowledge in our head will never be enough. It's only when we can rest in what we don't know that we can fully experience the love and presence of God with us:

We may not know the purpose of His ways, but we can experience the power of His love.

CLOSING MEDITATION

As we close our week together, I invite you to return to the practice of resting in God's presence. **You can use the prompts from Session 2, Day 3 (pages 67–68), or meditate on Psalm 131:1-2, included here.**

If you choose to spend time with this psalm, begin by reading the passage slowly. If you've ever rocked a child to sleep, imagine the rhythm of your body and breath as you settle and feel peace. You are that child to God, and you can rest in His peace. Stay in that space as long as you can, simply releasing what you don't know while embracing what God wants to provide: a powerful experience of His love.

My heart is not proud, LORD,
  my eyes are not haughty;
I do not concern myself with great matters
  or things too wonderful for me.
But I have calmed and quieted myself,
  I am like a weaned child with its mother;
  like a weaned child I am content.

PSALM 131:1-2

THE WORK OF PATIENCE

Kairos moments help define our destiny, and they are critical intersections as we live out our calling to bear witness to the grace of Jesus, to carry the kingdom of God with us, to allow blessing to flow through us in whatever plot twist God has next.

NOT WHAT I SIGNED UP FOR, PAGE 118

Nothing tests our patience like an unknown timeline, especially when we are living in a season we didn't expect. But seasons of waiting also present an opportunity: They are an invitation for us to grow in humility, surrender control, and seek God's mercy and help in ways we may have never experienced. This week we'll discover Joseph's rigorous trust in God, a trust that sustained him even when all hope seemed lost.

 MAIN POINT

One of our deepest expressions of faith is trusting God enough to continue moving forward, even in circumstances we don't understand.

 RECAP

Look over last week's homework. Share reflections from what you learned during your daily studies, particularly if you had a revelation about what God has taught you through difficult circumstances in the past.

Tune in to video session 4: "The Work of Patience"

VIDEO NOTES

1. Jesus calls it *blessed* when we are out of breath and out of options.

2. Trusting the opportunities in front of us takes upward, inward, and outward energy.

3. Jesus calls us *blessed* when we mourn.

4. Trusting in our tears connects us more deeply to what is broken and vulnerable, both in us and in our world.

OPENING GROUP CONVERSATION

1. Share about a moment that seemed insignificant at the time but ended up being an important part of your story. How do you see God's hand in that memory?

2. In the video teaching, we learn how being present in our lives is required to make us more aware of God's presence with us. Last week, you may have followed the challenge to become more aware of God in your day. Place a check mark next to the statement below that best summarizes your awareness of God during a normal day:

   ☐ I almost always pray or talk to God throughout the day and experience Christ through daily spiritual practices.

   ☐ If I'm struggling or stressed, I usually remember to pray and ask for help.

   ☐ I generally don't think to have conversations with God, especially when I'm busy.

   ☐ I try to get to church and Bible study, and that's the extent of it for me.

It's incredibly encouraging when we share with one another how God speaks to each one of us, so if you have grown in this area recently or even this week, share with the group how you experience God's presence and voice in your life:

📖 TO THE WORD TOGETHER

Let's go to a few passages that illuminate what rigorous trust looks like and how we might live into it ourselves.

1. **Read from Genesis 40:**

> [The cup-bearer and baker] remained in prison for quite some time, and the captain of the guard assigned them to Joseph, who looked after them.
>
> While they were in prison, Pharaoh's cup-bearer and baker each had a dream one night, and each dream had its own meaning. When Joseph saw them the next morning, he noticed that they both looked upset. "Why do you look so worried today?" he asked them.
>
> And they replied, "We both had dreams last night, but no one can tell us what they mean."
>
> "Interpreting dreams is God's business," Joseph replied. "Go ahead and tell me your dreams."
>
> **GENESIS 40:4-8, NLT**

   a. What details do you notice in this section of Joseph's story?

   b. Outside this passage, what have we seen about the ways Joseph maximized his opportunities?

c. What do you think gave Joseph, who was enslaved, suffering, and far from home, the ability to be both humble and confident in his circumstances?

2. Now let's see how Joseph's experiences relate to how we, in Christ, are called to live. **Read aloud together the following passage:**

> For what we preach is not ourselves, but Jesus Christ as Lord, and ourselves as your servants for Jesus' sake. For God, who said, "Let light shine out of darkness," made his light shine in our hearts to give us the light of the knowledge of God's glory displayed in the face of Christ.
>
> But we have this treasure in jars of clay to show that this all-surpassing power is from God and not from us. We are hard pressed on every side, but not crushed; perplexed, but not in despair; persecuted, but not abandoned; struck down, but not destroyed. We always carry around in our body the death of Jesus, so that the life of Jesus may also be revealed in our body. For we who are alive are always being given over to death for Jesus' sake, so that his life may also be revealed in our mortal body. So then, death is at work in us, but life is at work in you.
>
> 2 CORINTHIANS 4:5-12

a. As believers, what are we called to preach and why?

b. Based on this passage, what does the apostle Paul think we should expect out of life?

c. Why would we consider this good news?

3. Continue reading the passage:

> Therefore we do not lose heart. Though outwardly we are wasting away, yet inwardly we are being renewed day by day. For our light and momentary troubles are achieving for us an eternal glory that far outweighs them all. So we fix our eyes not on what is seen, but on what is unseen, since what is seen is temporary, but what is unseen is eternal.
>
> 2 CORINTHIANS 4:16-18

a. Looking at this entire passage, what do you think are the unseen things we are called to fix our eyes upon? How does that change how we view our circumstances today?

APPLICATION

Today we've focused on the opportunities God presents to us in life and how we can experience Him in any circumstance. This week, we will also look at the purpose of tears in our stories.

1. Growing up in your family, was it acceptable to experience negative emotions (sadness, anger, etc.)? How have your earliest experiences with negative emotions shaped you today?

2. Can you think of a time when you cried though you didn't want to? What was behind the tears? Why do you think vulnerability is hard for people?

3. Have you experienced significant grief in your life? When you think of that time, what helped? What didn't? How has grief changed you? (Remember, grief can follow loss of any kind, as we will talk about in chapter 8 of *Not What I Signed Up For*. Death brings one form of grief, but there are other losses we must grieve.)

👤 YOUR ONE THING

As the group closes, take two minutes to record one key takeaway from this session.

What words or ideas do you want to hang on to as you go into this week?

A CLOSING PRAYER

God, give us faith to believe that You're at work in our stories.
God, give us faith to believe Your intentions are good.
God, give us faith to believe . . . You.

We ask for the joy that comes from Your presence,
the confidence that comes from Your acceptance,
the healing that comes with Your mercy,

and the great blessing of Your love.

Grant us the humility to serve others like You do
and the trust to believe that Your mercy covers our weaknesses
and that Your powerful grace overcomes our failings. Amen.

ON YOUR OWN

DAILY STUDY

SESSION 4

DAY 1

GETTING UNSTUCK

When we find ourselves in circumstances we didn't expect and would never have asked for, we naturally look for a quick exit—or at least a way to bypass our discomfort.

> Getting stuck is a natural response in our unexpected seasons. We want to fight the world, to hold on to the hurt and grief and to force time to stop until everything is made right again—or we long to pull the covers over our heads as a way to tune out what feels unmanageable. But neither response will actually give us what we need in this season: the ability to stay present and engaged exactly where we are.
>
> *NOT WHAT I SIGNED UP FOR*, PAGES 114–115

As we turn our attention to Joseph's transition into prison, we would find it understandable if he got stuck in his own pain or resentment. Yet somehow Joseph made the most of even the worst circumstances. What gives a person that kind of resilience and strength? This week, we are going to take a good look at what tends to get us stuck—and what it looks like to live the real and redeemed way, even when it seems as if nothing is going our way.

REFLECT

1. Read Genesis 39–41. While reading this portion of Joseph's story, take note of every time you see Joseph seize an opportunity.

One temptation in a difficult season is to allow our pain to overshadow the good of any other experience. We may be tempted to believe that while we are hurting, isolated, or uncertain, we are disqualified from having any purpose or influence. We may think we can't do or bring anything to the world that matters.

Friend, that is untrue. That's a lie designed to keep you stuck and isolated. If you resonate with this description, this will be an important day in your study. We are going to focus on what it looks like to give each day to the Lord and trust Him with it, no matter what. **Let's start by reviewing a few verses about what we can expect from God today:**

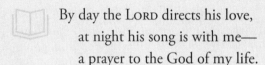

By day the Lord directs his love,
    at night his song is with me—
    a prayer to the God of my life.
PSALM 42:8

The whole earth is filled with awe at your wonders;
    where morning dawns, where evening fades,
    you call forth songs of joy.
PSALM 65:8

Morning by morning he dispenses his justice,
    and every new day he does not fail,
    yet the unrighteous know no shame.
ZEPHANIAH 3:5

Satisfy us in the morning with your unfailing love,
    that we may sing for joy and be glad all our days.
PSALM 90:14

Let the morning bring me word of your unfailing love,
    for I have put my trust in you.
Show me the way I should go,
    for to you I entrust my life.
PSALM 143:8

Yet this I call to mind
and therefore I have hope:

Because of the LORD's great love
we are not consumed,
for his compassions never fail.
They are new every morning;
great is your faithfulness.

LAMENTATIONS 3:21-23

2. Now read them over again and make a list of what God promises to do each day/ each morning:

3. Let's look at the righteous response to God's promises. What are the responses of the authors of the final three passages?

4. Now read this challenge from Colossians 3:

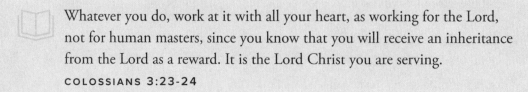

Whatever you do, work at it with all your heart, as working for the Lord, not for human masters, since you know that you will receive an inheritance from the Lord as a reward. It is the Lord Christ you are serving.

COLOSSIANS 3:23-24

a. If you were going to make a to-do list for today based on these verses, what would be on it?

-

-

-

-

CLOSING MEDITATION

Sometimes the most important thing you can do when you're stuck is to figure out what you *can* do, no matter how small—and call that good. Jesus said if we have faith as small as a mustard seed, nothing will be impossible for us (Matthew 17:20). Friend, even if your faith feels so tiny and the obstacles seem insurmountable, you can still praise God. Even if you don't feel like it, you can still praise God. If you can't find your own words today, I'm including a beautiful prayer, often attributed to St. Francis of Assisi, that can be used daily:

Lord, make me an instrument of your peace.
Where there is hatred, let me sow love;
where there is injury, pardon;
where there is doubt, faith;

where there is despair, hope;

where there is darkness, light;

where there is sadness, joy.

O Divine Master, grant that I may not so much seek

to be consoled as to console;

to be understood as to understand;

to be loved as to love.

For it is in giving that we receive;

it is in pardoning that we are pardoned;

and it is in dying that we are born to eternal life.

Amen.[1]

READ

Chapter 7, *Not What I Signed Up For*

Use this space to capture any key phrases or takeaways from the chapter that you want to remember:

"A pessimist sees the difficulty in every opportunity; an optimist sees the opportunity in every difficulty."[2] Though it's likely Joseph struggled to maintain perspective at least occasionally during his many years of captivity, his faith in God allowed him to look forward in hope. As we continue to wait with Joseph, still contemplating the long space between his dreams as a teenager and his elevation to power in Egypt, we have the opportunity to enter into the waiting with eyes ready to see what good can arise out of even the worst of circumstances.

 ## REFLECT

In chapter 7 of *Not What I Signed Up For*, we contemplate the three directions that Joseph looked as he trusted God's promises to him. Those perspectives are available to us as well. **Let's use each of those directions as our reflection for today:**

- ### Upward: the opportunity to engage God

  I have a simple upward practice: I read the Psalms until a verse or phrase stands out on the page. Sometimes it's the first line; sometimes it's a few chapters in. Then I write that one verse or phrase into my journal. The physical act of copying the verse in my own hand is a way to claim the truth, promise, or encouragement. I then write a short prayer underneath that, asking God for whatever comes to mind from that verse. Rather than allowing my flip-flopping heart or fickle emotions to lead my time with God, I start from His Word so that I can posture my soul upward, and then work inward from there.

  NOT WHAT I SIGNED UP FOR, PAGES 123–124

- ### Inward: the opportunity to engage our inner world

  As a practice, I teach [my leadership teams] a posture—putting their hands together in a prayer position, thumbs touching the center of their chests. This is a heart posture, where we are physically connecting our hands and hearts, reminding our bodies that we are not just mechanically surviving this life but that our souls can dwell with us in the present moment. In this position, we can acknowledge our needs and ask God to meet them in a way that allows us to be an instrument for His plans and purposes.

NOT WHAT I SIGNED UP FOR, PAGES 124–125

- ### Outward: the opportunity to engage the outer world

  When Joseph spoke with the cupbearer and the baker, he was not wrapped up in his own pain. Because he trusted God, he had humility, and that humility allowed him to be present. And the present is where we notice things. One morning, he asked his two fellow prisoners, "Why are your faces so sad today?" (Genesis 40:7, NASB). Notice this small but important detail: Only people fully engaged in the present and confident that their presence matters will notice something as small as a facial expression and then try to do something to help.

  NOT WHAT I SIGNED UP FOR, PAGE 125

1. Try this for yourself. **Select one of the following passages to use as a starting point: Psalm 1, Psalm 16, Psalm 37, or Psalm 86.**

2. **Copy the phrase or verse that stands out to you today:**

3. Now turn to the inward posture. **Press your open hands together, with thumbs touching the center of your chest. What do you need from God today? Write a short prayer of request here:**

 ## CLOSING MEDITATION

After fixing our eyes on Jesus and then taking a moment to acknowledge our needs to God, we are ready for our outward posture, which enables us to engage the world around us.

What opportunities do you need to trust God with today? Where (or for whom) do you want to show up fully present? Ask God to reveal those opportunities and help you be an instrument of His peace and love in those places.

THE POWER OF LAMENT

What do we do with our pain, confusion, or just *blah* days that color our life as humans? If you've only experienced a "look on the bright side" faith, you may not know if it's acceptable to be transparent with God—and even if you want to invite Jesus into your sorrow, you may not know *how*. Today let's look at the biblical concept of lament—the why, what, and how of lament in our spiritual practices.

 REFLECT

Why lament?

Lament is the way we engage with God about our pain, disappointment, and confusion. Complicated emotions like these can tempt us to isolate or distance ourselves from Him, especially when we don't "feel" Him near us. Lament is the vehicle that leads us back into communion with our heavenly Father.

What is lament?

Lament is the way we pray to God with our pain. There are four aspects of lament:[3]

1. **Turn:** bringing our specific pain to God
2. **Complain:** naming what is wrong
3. **Ask:** seeking God's mercy and deliverance; asking for help
4. **Trust:** making the active choice to trust God

How to lament

1. **Read these verses from Psalm 22. Underline the verses where the psalmist is complaining, circle the phrases where he is asking, and place a star next to the places where the psalmist expresses his trust in God.**

My God, my God, why have you forsaken me?
　　Why are you so far from saving me,
　　so far from my cries of anguish?
My God, I cry out by day, but you do not answer,
　　by night, but I find no rest.

Yet you are enthroned as the Holy One;
　　you are the one Israel praises.
In you our ancestors put their trust;
　　they trusted and you delivered them.
To you they cried out and were saved;
　　in you they trusted and were not put to shame.

But I am a worm and not a man,
　　scorned by everyone, despised by the people.
All who see me mock me;
　　they hurl insults, shaking their heads.
"He trusts in the LORD," they say,
　　"let the LORD rescue him.
Let him deliver him,
　　since he delights in him."

Yet you brought me out of the womb;
　　you made me trust in you, even at my mother's breast.
From birth I was cast on you;
　　from my mother's womb you have been my God.

PSALM 22:1-10

The Bible does not shy away from times when we suffer. The earliest followers of Jesus faced troubles of all kinds, and the encouragement given to them applies to us today.

2. Read the following verses, underlining the word *patient*:

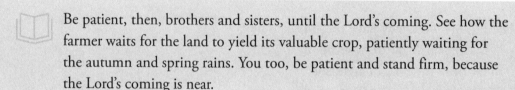

Be patient, then, brothers and sisters, until the Lord's coming. See how the farmer waits for the land to yield its valuable crop, patiently waiting for the autumn and spring rains. You too, be patient and stand firm, because the Lord's coming is near.

JAMES 5:7-8

Love must be sincere. Hate what is evil; cling to what is good. Be devoted to one another in love. Honor one another above yourselves. Never be lacking in zeal, but keep your spiritual fervor, serving the Lord. Be joyful in hope, patient in affliction, faithful in prayer.

ROMANS 12:9-12

Much of our character is revealed during tests of waiting. For Joseph, testing looked like long years in prison, where he knew nothing about his family's well-being, where the dreams he once had seemed long dead, and where all he could cling to was his faith in God. For us, it might not look like a literal prison, but we may feel imprisoned by obstacles or difficulties we must endure. Waiting often reveals both strengths and weaknesses in our character.

3. When you think about being patient in affliction, which of the following responses sounds most like you? Circle the one that fits best.

a. I have been through difficult trials in my life, and I've learned how to trust God through them.

b. I am in a difficult trial right now, and I have some days when I trust God and some when I doubt His goodness.

c. I have not learned how to trust God with hard things.

d. Other: _____.

4. Regardless of what trials you've been through or what you've learned about God so far in life, you will never outgrow your need to practice being honest *and* trusting God as you pray. **Practice your own lament today, using Psalm 22 as a guide.**

   a. **Turn:** Spend a moment or two breathing deeply and actively turning your whole self toward God's presence.

   b. **Complain:** What do you specifically need to share with God today? What feels confusing, unfair, hurtful, or disappointing?

   c. **Ask:** What would you like God to do for you?

d. **Trust:** We rest our case with God when we end our prayer with confidence, knowing He will respond to our requests. Copy down the words from Psalm 13:5-6 in the space below or write your own version:

 ## CLOSING MEDITATION

Father, I thank You that You hear my prayer. Thank You that through Jesus Christ, I can have the peace of Your presence with me, regardless of my trial. Holy Spirit, would You intercede for me, bringing me the deep comfort of Your presence and the counsel of Your wisdom until I rest again at the end of this day. Amen.

MAKING PEACE WITH LOSS

READ

Chapter 8, Not What I Signed Up For

Use this space to capture any key phrases or takeaways from the chapter that you want to remember:

Grief is as much a part of life as love. But allowing ourselves the space needed to grieve, to work through the uncontrollable pain of it, takes courage. Yet God makes it clear that He is near to those who mourn, and He will comfort them (Matthew 5:4). You will go through the "valley of the shadow of death," but you will not go alone (Psalm 23:4, ESV).

Embracing and honoring your grief is the final stage in learning to trust God in your painful, unexpected season, and it's the longest part of the journey. As you mourn, it's critical to engage with God about what you've lost, what you miss, and what you grieve. Even if the loss is something you chose or something that's ultimately good (like your children growing up), and even if what you've left behind comes with many new and good things, it's still loss. It's still the end of a season, the death of a dream, the loss of a relationship.

NOT WHAT I SIGNED UP FOR, PAGE 137

 REFLECT

1. On a scale of 1 to 10 (1 being least comfortable and 10 being most comfortable), how comfortable are you "embracing and honoring" your grief?

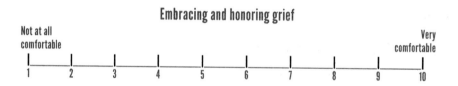

2. If you scored a 7 or above, what have you learned that helps you to embrace and honor grief?

3. If you scored below a 7, what do you think blocks you from your grief? Circle all that apply.

   a. I am scared of what would happen if I actually let myself feel that pain.
   b. I don't think I've had any significant loss or haven't been able to name that loss.
   c. I don't want to feel grief, so I try to skip it and stuff it away.
   d. Other:_____.

We began the process of honest lament yesterday in our homework. If you've begun the rigorous work of bringing your lament to God and trusting Him with it, you can wait with confidence for the Lord to hear your cry. And if you feel stuck in your grief today, perhaps a gentle act of self-care would be to simply read the following verses, adapted and personalized for you. Allow the mercy of God to fill you today.

4. Write your name on each of the following blank lines as a personal letter from God to you:

Be glad and rejoice with all your heart, _____!
The LORD has taken away your punishment.
ZEPHANIAH 3:14-15

_____, the LORD your God is with you,
   the Mighty Warrior who saves.
He will take great delight in you, _____;
   . . . [and] will rejoice over you with singing.
ZEPHANIAH 3:17

Do not fear,_____, for I have redeemed you;
   I have summoned you by name; you are mine.
ISAIAH 43:1

_____, you will grieve, but your grief will turn to joy.
JOHN 16:20

_____, the Father himself loves you because you have loved me
and have believed that I came from God.
JOHN 16:27

_____, take heart! I have overcome the world.
JOHN 16:33

God has spoken it, and every word He says is true. Your role is simply to grow in
your belief that all of these promises are true for you.

 ## CLOSING MEDITATION

Select one of the previous passages that you've personalized with your name. Write it
on a sticky note and pray it to God. Then place the note somewhere that you'll see it
first thing each morning this week.

NAMING OUR GRIEF

We've spent the last week studying waiting—waiting like Joseph waited for his deliverance, waiting like Jesus until "his hour had come" (John 13:1, ESV). We wait in life for many things, and often we grieve while we wait. We grieve the loss of our own dreams; we grieve the gap between our expectations and our reality. We grieve the passing of time; we grieve our aging bodies. We grieve for relationships that were, for relationships that are not enough, for relationships that are over. We grieve our past, and sometimes we grieve the future that never will be. Yet we do not have to grieve like those with no hope (1 Thessalonians 4:13). We grieve but with the comfort and presence of God over our grief, just as Joseph experienced when he named his children:

> Before the years of famine came, two sons were born to Joseph by Asenath daughter of Potiphera, priest of On. Joseph named his firstborn Manasseh and said, "It is because God has made me forget all my trouble and all my father's household." The second son he named Ephraim and said, "It is because God has made me fruitful in the land of my suffering."
> **GENESIS 41:50-52**

God's promise of comfort extends to us today. "He heals the brokenhearted and binds up their wounds" (Psalm 147:3). He even tracks our tears: "You have kept record of my days of wandering. You have stored my tears in your bottle" (Psalm 56:8, CEV). In chapter 8 of *Not What I Signed Up For*, you were invited to present your case to God and then to rest with Him as He heals you.

REFLECT

Today we will finish the session with a creative exercise. All you need is a bottle or vase and a pen and paper, but you can make this as personal as you'd like. Grab a beautiful vessel, paints or markers, or any other art material that helps you express yourself.

1. Use the pen and paper to present your case to God. You can write out specific areas or relationships in your life that you need to grieve. Put one on each slip of paper.

2. Pick up each slip, one at a time. As you read what you wrote, roll up that paper. Imagine carrying that loss to the feet of Jesus. Place the paper into the bottle or vase, and pray, *God, I rest my case with you.* Repeat with each slip of paper until you've transferred them all to the bottle.

3. Keep your vessel for the duration of this study. Anytime you feel yourself going back to that loss, you can remember resting your case with God and giving the burden to Him. You can add to the bottle if more burdens come to mind, and use your own prayer or the one I've written for you below.

CLOSING MEDITATION

Here is a simple prayer that I offer in case you need help finding the words that help you surrender.

A PRAYER FOR WHEN YOU ARE READY TO REST

Well, God,

I claim that I've staked my life on Your promises,
but I keep forgetting to believe them.

It's easier to find a million ways to fix it,

to self-care and self-cope

and self-protect

until I'm exhausted and brittle with the effort.

So, Lord, for the millionth time,

I surrender again.

I rest my case with You.

I give up on getting it right and give in to
       Your grace.

Help me rest here a little while.

And thanks in advance—

we both know I'll be here again.

Amen, anyway.

NOT WHAT I SIGNED UP FOR, **PAGE 151**

Hallelujah to our God who saves; who will always come to our rescue; who binds our wounds, heals our hearts, carries our burdens, and gives us the great gift of hope and a future!

THE POWER OF REDEMPTION

Redemption always centers on God and extends beyond ourselves. God holds together a bigger plan than the one we each live in. We are in a long, linked chain of relationships—those who have gone before us, those who will come after us. The choices we make today—to bless or to curse, to choose life or to choose death—eventually have ripple effects through our own family history.

NOT WHAT I SIGNED UP FOR, PAGE 184

This week we turn our attention toward redemption—what it is, how we experience it, and how it transforms us. Redemption is God's way of using everything in our lives—even the worst pain—to lead us deeper into His love. Redemption is often accompanied by both repentance and forgiveness. As we take a front-row seat to the way redemption plays out in Joseph's story, we'll ask God to show us how His loving hand is also directing our redemptive stories.

 ## MAIN POINT

Redemption through Christ is God's extension of blessing to us and the promise of the Holy Spirit for us.

 ## RECAP

Look over last week's homework. **Share your reflections as you consider Joseph's story to this point. What's an insight or reflection related to the way you've been processing your own period of waiting?**

Tune in to video session 5: "The Power of Redemption"

 **VIDEO NOTES**

1. Redemption is what happens when love hits pain.

2. God's kindness is meant to lead you to repentance.

3. Redemption sets you free from blame and shame.

4. We all have to make the daily decision to live in the redeemed story of our lives.

👥 OPENING GROUP CONVERSATION

1. How did your family handle conflict and forgiveness as you were growing up? How is your current life shaped by that?

2. In your own words, what does redemption mean? Do you have an example of it from your life? If so and you feel comfortable doing so, share it with your group.

3. If you currently have an unredeemed storyline in your life, bring it to mind and then answer the following:

    a. When I think about _____, what would redemption look like (e.g., restoration, reconciliation, etc.)?

b. If nothing in the outward circumstances of this situation changed, what would redemption look like (e.g., freedom from regret, the ability to forgive, freedom from anxiety or the impulse to analyze the situation, etc.)?

📖 TO THE WORD TOGETHER

Redemption almost always brings with it repentance and forgiveness. Repentance is not necessary for us to forgive but is almost always needed (from both parties) in order to reconcile or restore relationship. Repentance is not just saying sorry. It's changing one's mind toward God's way, in both words and action.

1. Read the following passage, which contains a strong rebuke from John the Baptist, a prophet who foretold the coming of Christ. John the Baptist taught and baptized in the Judean wilderness. When doing so, he often called out the Pharisees and Sadducees, religious leaders of the day, for their fake piety. In other words, they looked good on the outside but were prideful and stubborn on the inside:

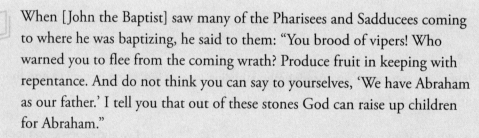

When [John the Baptist] saw many of the Pharisees and Sadducees coming to where he was baptizing, he said to them: "You brood of vipers! Who warned you to flee from the coming wrath? Produce fruit in keeping with repentance. And do not think you can say to yourselves, 'We have Abraham as our father.' I tell you that out of these stones God can raise up children for Abraham."

MATTHEW 3:7-9

a. What does John say is the true sign of repentance?

b. What excuse from these religious leaders does he call out? What are some excuses you've made (or seen others make) to avoid real repentance?

2. Real repentance always produces fruit. Make a list of the kind of "fruit" you've experienced from real repentance, either in yourself or in others.

Before reading a few highlights from the brothers' reunion with Joseph, let's take a closer look at his brother Judah. He was the one who suggested that the brothers sell Joseph into slavery rather than have his blood on their own hands. (Slavery was still a death sentence, but it was a nice way to try to shift the guilt elsewhere.)

At some point Judah married a Canaanite woman, with whom he had three sons. The oldest married Tamar, and after his death, the second-born son married her, according to the customs of the time. He also died. Years later Judah reneged on his promise to Tamar to give her to his youngest son in marriage. With few options as a widow, Tamar orchestrated a dramatic intervention that led Judah, perhaps for the first time, to show remorse for his actions in life (Genesis 38).

That reorientation likely drove Judah's maturity when Jacob resisted sending his sons back to Egypt for food because Joseph (whom the brothers didn't yet recognize) had demanded they bring Benjamin with them:

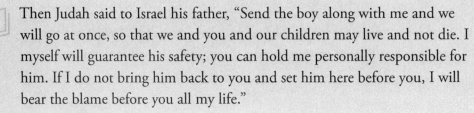

> Then Judah said to Israel his father, "Send the boy along with me and we will go at once, so that we and you and our children may live and not die. I myself will guarantee his safety; you can hold me personally responsible for him. If I do not bring him back to you and set him here before you, I will bear the blame before you all my life."
>
> **GENESIS 43:8-9**

Once Jacob's sons returned to Egypt and paid for their food, Joseph had one of his managers plant his silver cup in Benjamin's sack and then chase down the brothers as they returned home. Once back at the palace, the manager searched everyone's sack. When he "found" the cup in Benjamin's sack, the brothers felt despair. After all, they'd guaranteed Benjamin's safe return. When taken before Joseph, Judah proclaimed that all the brothers would be his slaves.

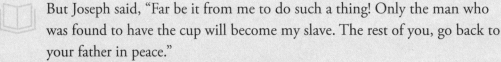

> But Joseph said, "Far be it from me to do such a thing! Only the man who was found to have the cup will become my slave. The rest of you, go back to your father in peace."
>
> Then Judah went up to him and said: "Pardon your servant, my lord, let me speak a word to my lord. Do not be angry with your servant, though you are equal to Pharaoh himself. My lord asked his servants, 'Do you have a father or a brother?' And we answered, 'We have an aged father, and there is a young son born to him in his old age. His brother is dead, and he is the only one of his mother's sons left, and his father loves him.'
>
> "Then you said to your servants, 'Bring him down to me so I can see him for myself.' And we said to my lord, 'The boy cannot leave his father; if he leaves him, his father will die.' But you told your servants, 'Unless your

youngest brother comes down with you, you will not see my face again.' When we went back to your servant my father, we told him what my lord had said. . . .

"Your servant guaranteed the boy's safety to my father. I said, 'If I do not bring him back to you, I will bear the blame before you, my father, all my life!'

"Now then, please let your servant remain here as my lord's slave in place of the boy, and let the boy return with his brothers. How can I go back to my father if the boy is not with me? No! Do not let me see the misery that would come on my father."

GENESIS 44:17-24, 32-34

Notice how Judah's importance in his family was further established by his role in settling Jacob and his sons in Egypt and later in Jacob's final blessing to him.

With the two sons who had been born to Joseph in Egypt, the members of Jacob's family, which went to Egypt, were seventy in all.

Now Jacob sent Judah ahead of him to Joseph to get directions to Goshen. When they arrived in the region of Goshen, Joseph had his chariot made ready and went to Goshen to meet his father Israel. As soon as Joseph appeared before him, he threw his arms around his father and wept for a long time.

GENESIS 46:27-29

Then Jacob called for his sons and said: "Gather around so I can tell you what will happen to you in days to come.

"Assemble and listen, sons of Jacob;
    listen to your father Israel. . . .

"Judah, your brothers will praise you;
    your hand will be on the neck of your enemies;
    your father's sons will bow down to you.

147

You are a lion's cub, Judah;
    you return from the prey, my son.
Like a lion he crouches and lies down,
    like a lioness—who dares to rouse him?
The scepter will not depart from Judah,
    nor the ruler's staff from between his feet,
until he to whom it belongs shall come
    and the obedience of the nations shall be his."

GENESIS 49:1-2, 8-10

3. How would you trace the movement of Judah's life, from self-centered to other-centered living?

4. What does real repentance look like in Judah's story?

5. What is the fruit of repentance and redemption in Judah's life?

One more note: Jacob's prophecy held true—from Judah's lineage, many generations later, came King David, and eventually, Jesus Christ, who is called "the Lion of the tribe of Judah" (Revelation 5:5).

APPLICATION

1. How would you explain the relationship between repentance and redemption?

2. What do you think it means to "produce fruit in keeping with repentance" (Matthew 3:8)? What does it mean for you when it comes to your response to someone who has sinned against you?

3. What is your understanding of the difference between forgiveness and reconciliation?

YOUR ONE THING

As the group closes, take two minutes to record one key takeaway from this session.

What words or ideas do you want to hang on to as you go into this week?

A CLOSING PRAYER

God, give us faith to believe You're at work in our stories.
God, give us faith to believe Your intentions are good.
God, give us faith to believe . . . You.

We ask for the joy that comes from Your presence,
the confidence that comes from Your acceptance,
the healing that comes with Your mercy,

and the great blessing of Your love.

Grant us the humility to serve others like You do
and the trust to believe that Your mercy covers our weaknesses
and that Your powerful grace overcomes our failings. Amen.

ON YOUR OWN

DAILY STUDY

SESSION 5

CHANGING DIRECTIONS

Today we will read Genesis 42, a chapter that hits us with the reality of redemption: It's a process. As much as we might like to skip ahead and resolve Joseph's story, his slow and deliberate reveal to his brothers is necessary to expose the truth. Likewise for us, sometimes the slow process of reflection leads us to repentance.

> The Greek word translated *repent* essentially means "to change one's mind." In the New Testament, that repentance is a change of mind, a moral reorientation toward God.[1] It is the love of God that reveals redemption in our stories, and it is also the love of God that uses all the materials of life to help us leave our childish ways behind, to grow up into His love, to change our minds toward God in repentance.
>
> *NOT WHAT I SIGNED UP FOR*, PAGES 156–157

 REFLECT

Read Genesis 42. As you do, consider what time and tests revealed in Joseph's story— and what they might reveal in yours.

1. How do the brothers interpret what is happening to them in this chapter?

2. Based on his response, how do you think Jacob interprets what is happening to him in this chapter?

3. The slow reveal gives us a glimpse into the beliefs the brothers and their father, Jacob, have about God. **Turn back to page 92 in this study. In your own suffering, what false beliefs about God are you tempted to hold?**

Recall that repentance essentially means to change our minds or disposition toward God. Our false beliefs about God are often revealed in our distress, which means that we will often need to repent during these times. We are called to "be transformed by the renewing of [our] mind[s]" (Romans 12:2), and one of the best ways to do that is to bring our false beliefs into God's healing presence and then replace those lies with the truth.

4. **Underline all the promises of God for you listed in the psalm below:**

Hear me, LORD, and answer me,
    for I am poor and needy.
Guard my life, for I am faithful to you;
    save your servant who trusts in you.
You are my God; have mercy on me, Lord,
    for I call to you all day long.
Bring joy to your servant, Lord,
    for I put my trust in you.

You, Lord, are forgiving and good,
    abounding in love to all who call to you.
Hear my prayer, LORD;
    listen to my cry for mercy.
When I am in distress, I call to you,
    because you answer me.

Among the gods there is none like you, Lord;
  no deeds can compare with yours.
All the nations you have made
  will come and worship before you, Lord;
  they will bring glory to your name.
For you are great and do marvelous deeds;
  you alone are God.

Teach me your way, LORD,
  that I may rely on your faithfulness;
give me an undivided heart,
  that I may fear your name.
I will praise you, Lord my God, with all my heart;
  I will glorify your name forever.
For great is your love toward me;
  you have delivered me from the depths,
  from the realm of the dead.

PSALM 86:1-13

 ## CLOSING MEDITATION

Look back at your underlined notes from Psalm 86. **Write a prayer of declaration about who God is as a way to turn away (repent) from any false beliefs you are carrying. I wrote the first one for you:**

*Lord, I turn away from the idea that You don't see me, for great is
    Your love for me!*

Lord, I turn away from _____ because _____.

READ

Chapter 9, *Not What I Signed Up For*

Use this space to capture any key phrases or takeaways from the chapter that you want to remember:

Our big emotions—pain, grief, regret, shame—are complicated. They are often hard to separate from one another, and we often swing wildly between shame (*What is happening to me is all my fault* and *I am not worth loving/seeing*) and anger (*What is happening to me is because of this person/these people; I am powerless; I am the victim*). Over time these big, complicated emotions can become burdens that weigh us down, making it difficult for us to move forward.

REFLECT

1. Joseph's brothers believed God was punishing them. Jacob believed all of life was against him. **When you are operating from these kinds of belief statements, what fruit tends to be produced in your life?**

   Friend, remember that regardless of what has brought you to this season, redemption is the way out. If you are stuck in shame or anger, believing in God's redemptive work can get you unstuck.

2. We've camped out in Joseph's life to see what choosing the redeemed life looks like. **What are some of the choices Joseph made that reveal his decision to stay in the redeemed story?**

3. What are some choices you can make today to stay in a redeemed story?

CLOSING MEDITATION

One of the great gifts of God's healing presence is the ability to see things rightly—to have the wisdom to release what you cannot control and activate what you can. Let's close today by breathing deeply in God's presence, handing over any burdens into His care; releasing any guilt, shame, or regret; and stepping out in the confidence of His presence and love.

1. Take a breath and relax your body.
2. Take as long as you need in God's presence to release your burdens for today. Imagine each burden like a package that you bring and lay before God's throne of mercy. Imagine the shape of each one as you feel the weight move from your hands and into His loving presence.
3. Now, while still in His presence, allow God to fill your hands with the gifts He has for you today. Receive His love, patience, compassion, wisdom, and righteousness. Thank God for any specific gifts you sense the Holy Spirit filling you with today:

Go with God's peace and confidence into your day, knowing that He sees you, He loves you, and He is with you!

BEAUTY FROM ASHES

"Redemption is perhaps the greatest promise, the greatest hope of our humanity" (*Not What I Signed Up For*, page 176). After the waiting and the testing, after Judah makes his plea and demonstrates sacrificial love for his brothers, Joseph has seen enough, and the redemption story is magnificent.

Read Genesis 45:

Joseph could stand it no longer. There were many people in the room, and he said to his attendants, "Out, all of you!" So he was alone with his brothers when he told them who he was. Then he broke down and wept. He wept so loudly the Egyptians could hear him, and word of it quickly carried to Pharaoh's palace.

"I am Joseph!" he said to his brothers. "Is my father still alive?" But his brothers were speechless! They were stunned to realize that Joseph was standing there in front of them. "Please, come closer," he said to them. So they came closer. And he said again, "I am Joseph, your brother, whom you sold into slavery in Egypt. But don't be upset, and don't be angry with yourselves for selling me to this place. It was God who sent me here ahead of you to preserve your lives. This famine that has ravaged the land for two years will last five more years, and there will be neither plowing nor harvesting. God has sent me ahead of you to keep you and your families alive and to preserve many survivors. So it was God who sent me here, not you! And he is the one who made me an adviser to Pharaoh—the manager of his entire palace and the governor of all Egypt.

"Now hurry back to my father and tell him, 'This is what your son Joseph says: God has made me master over all the land of Egypt. So come down to me immediately! You can live in the region of Goshen, where you can be near me with all your children and grandchildren, your flocks and herds, and everything you own. I will take care of you there, for there are still five years of famine ahead of us. Otherwise you, your household, and all your animals will starve.'"

Then Joseph added, "Look! You can see for yourselves, and so can my brother Benjamin, that I really am Joseph! Go tell my father of my honored position here in Egypt. Describe for him everything you have seen, and then bring my father here quickly." Weeping with joy, he embraced Benjamin, and Benjamin did the same. Then Joseph kissed each of his brothers and wept over them, and after that they began talking freely with him.

The news soon reached Pharaoh's palace: "Joseph's brothers have arrived!" Pharaoh and his officials were all delighted to hear this.

Pharaoh said to Joseph, "Tell your brothers, 'This is what you must do: Load your pack animals, and hurry back to the land of Canaan. Then get your father and all of your families, and return here to me. I will give you the very best land in Egypt, and you will eat from the best that the land produces.'"

Then Pharaoh said to Joseph, "Tell your brothers, 'Take wagons from the land of Egypt to carry your little children and your wives, and bring your father here. Don't worry about your personal belongings, for the best of all the land of Egypt is yours.'"

So the sons of Jacob did as they were told. Joseph provided them with wagons, as Pharaoh had commanded, and he gave them supplies for the journey. And he gave each of them new clothes—but to Benjamin he gave five changes of clothes and 300 pieces of silver. He also sent his father ten male donkeys loaded with the finest products of Egypt, and ten female donkeys loaded with grain and bread and other supplies he would need on his journey.

So Joseph sent his brothers off, and as they left, he called after them, "Don't quarrel about all this along the way!" And they left Egypt and returned to their father, Jacob, in the land of Canaan.

"Joseph is still alive!" they told him. "And he is governor of all the land of Egypt!" Jacob was stunned at the news—he couldn't believe it. But when they repeated to Jacob everything Joseph had told them, and when he saw the wagons Joseph had sent to carry him, their father's spirits revived.

Then Jacob exclaimed, "It must be true! My son Joseph is alive! I must go and see him before I die."

GENESIS 45, NLT

 REFLECT

1. How does Joseph comfort his brothers?

2. What is Pharaoh's response to the news that Joseph's family has appeared?

3. How did Jacob respond when he learned that Joseph was alive and well?

Do you remember our opening word on blessing—that blessing is always about what's happening through you? What a beautiful picture we have here of the ripple effects of Joseph's integrity and character. His view of God's work in his story enabled him to bless, not condemn, his brothers. His ability to lead with diligence and integrity in the "land of [his] suffering" (Genesis 41:52) bore fruit in the extravagant provision for his family, made possible by Pharaoh. And his return to his father revived Jacob's spirit.

When we persevere through the tests, when we continue to trust God even in our darkest days, we have no idea the future blessing that's coming to others through us for generations to come!

Now read the following passage written by the apostle Paul, who was no stranger to trouble. Underline the word *comfort* and circle the word *suffering*.

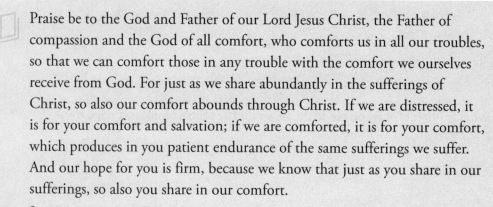

Praise be to the God and Father of our Lord Jesus Christ, the Father of compassion and the God of all comfort, who comforts us in all our troubles, so that we can comfort those in any trouble with the comfort we ourselves receive from God. For just as we share abundantly in the sufferings of Christ, so also our comfort abounds through Christ. If we are distressed, it is for your comfort and salvation; if we are comforted, it is for your comfort, which produces in you patient endurance of the same sufferings we suffer. And our hope for you is firm, because we know that just as you share in our sufferings, so also you share in our comfort.

2 CORINTHIANS 1:3-7

4. Where do we receive comfort?

5. What do we do with the comfort we receive?

6. What are these experiences of suffering and subsequent comfort meant to produce in us?

 **CLOSING MEDITATION**

Think of a time in your life when you received comfort from someone. **Now take a moment to thank God specifically for the person who comforted you.**

List a few experiences in your life that brought trouble or suffering but that you've seen God use as a way for you to comfort others.

-

-

-

As we view our own stories through God's redemptive lens, something miraculous happens: We grow in hope. We remember that even in our suffering, we know a God of all comfort. And if we will allow Him to comfort and heal us and to redeem every part of us, we will experience the blessing of comforting others and of seeing how God can bring beauty from ashes every single time.

As you rest in God's presence today, I invite you to write a simple prayer using this prompt:

God of all comfort, I receive Your comfort right now in these parts of my story: _____. I ask that You would give me [insert your request here]_____ in order that I might be a comfort to others. Holy Spirit, would You heal my pain and allow it to be used for Your purposes. Amen.

THE HOPE OF REDEMPTION

 READ

Chapter 10, Not What I Signed Up For

Use this space to capture any key phrases or takeaways from the chapter that you want to remember:

Redemption is all around us. It is the song waiting to be sung. But hearing that redemption song takes intentional listening—listening to our own stories and to what God is speaking to us through His Word. And it's often in the reflection from our own listening that we discover God's sovereign presence has always been with us.

REFLECT

Redemptive conversations spark hope, reveal blessing, and move us toward joy. Choose one of the prompts below to help you step into your redemption story. **Take a few minutes to journal about that question in the space provided.**

- What's the best thing you learned through one of your worst experiences?
- How has your character deepened through trials?
- What moments in your life that seemed ordinary at the time do you now know were key to the way God has shaped you?
- In what ways has your trust in God grown through difficult seasons?
- What have you learned about forgiveness?
- What have you learned about redemption?
- What have you learned about God's love? What promises have shaped your identity?
- First Peter 3:15 says that we should always be prepared to give an answer for the reason we have hope. Why do you have hope?

_____

_____

_____

_____

_____

_____

_____

_____

_____

_____

_____

_____

_____

_____

_____

 ## CLOSING MEDITATION

As you close your time of reflection, declare this promise of God, adapted from 1 Peter 1:18-19, as your prayer of praise:

God of all comfort, You paid a ransom so that I don't have to live an empty life. My stories are not meaningless, my suffering is not wasted—all because the precious blood of Christ has redeemed me. Help me to live in that truth today, full of the hope that comes from the living Christ, in whose name I pray. Amen.

LIVING RECONCILED

Hope begins in the dark, the stubborn hope that if you just show up and try to do the right thing, the dawn will come. You wait and watch and work: you don't give up.

ANNE LAMOTT, *BIRD BY BIRD: SOME INSTRUCTIONS ON WRITING AND LIFE*

As we trace the stories of redemption through the hills and valleys of our own journeys, we will be tempted to trip over the parts of our stories that we interpret as being unfinished. It's easy to get bogged down in the circumstances and worries that still concern us. But here's some amazing news: When we are in Christ, we share in the greatest redemption story of all—that of our salvation.

 REFLECT

1. Take a moment to remember this most important part of our story by reading the following passage on life apart from Christ:

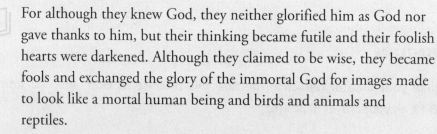

> For although they knew God, they neither glorified him as God nor gave thanks to him, but their thinking became futile and their foolish hearts were darkened. Although they claimed to be wise, they became fools and exchanged the glory of the immortal God for images made to look like a mortal human being and birds and animals and reptiles.
>
> Therefore God gave them over in the sinful desires of their hearts to sexual impurity for the degrading of their bodies with one another. They exchanged the truth about God for a lie, and worshiped and served created things rather than the Creator—who is forever praised. Amen.
>
> **ROMANS 1:21-25**

a. What happens to our thinking when we turn from God?

b. Before you came to Christ, in what ways did you find yourself worshiping and serving things other than God? (This could be anything you might have attached your identity to—career, appearance, material possessions, approval, etc.)

2. Now read on in Romans.

> God will credit righteousness—for us who believe in him who raised Jesus our Lord from the dead. He was delivered over to death for our sins and was raised to life for our justification.
>
> Therefore, since we have been justified through faith, we have peace with God through our Lord Jesus Christ, through whom we have gained access by faith into this grace in which we now stand. . . .
>
> Not only is this so, but we also boast in God through our Lord Jesus Christ, through whom we have now received reconciliation.
>
> **ROMANS 4:24–5:2, 11**

a. How do we become righteous?

To justify essentially means to "declare righteous," to "vindicate," or "to validate or prove to be right."[2] It is only through our faith in Christ—our faith that He is the One who makes us right before God—that we come to salvation.

b. What does our justification bring?

3. As we accept Christ by faith, we are reconciled to God. **Read the following verses from Romans 8, which illustrate some of the ways reconciliation changes our lives:**

The mind governed by the Spirit is life and peace.
VERSE 6

For those who are led by the Spirit of God are the children of God.
VERSE 14

Now if we are children, then we are heirs—heirs of God and co-heirs with Christ.
VERSE 17

The Spirit intercedes for God's people in accordance with the will of God.
VERSE 27

We know that in all things God works for the good of those who love him, who have been called according to his purpose.
VERSE 28

Christ Jesus who died—more than that, who was raised to life—is at the right hand of God and is also interceding for us.
VERSE 34

Who shall separate us from the love of Christ? Shall trouble or hardship or persecution or famine or nakedness or danger or sword? . . . No, in all these things we are more than conquerors through him who loved us.
VERSES 35, 37

a. From these verses, make a list of the realities of life in the Spirit:

 ## CLOSING MEDITATION

Even while some aspects of our stories remain unreconciled, the most important part *is* reconciled. Our hearts are reconciled to God, and nothing can separate us from that love. Our identities are secure. Our future is glorious. We live as children of the light now, and through the Spirit we've been given everything we need for a godly life. We are a redeemed and chosen people, and this is the source of our hope.

As you close this time, choose one (or more) of the benefits of your salvation to thank God for in your own prayer:

THE STORY OF SOVEREIGNTY

Unexpected seasons invite us to live in the mystery between the crucifix and the
resurrection. As we walk forward in our uncertainty, or look back and ask God to
redeem what's broken and painful, we need a way to frame our lives with room for
both the cross where Jesus died and the empty cross where we are revived, restored,
and refreshed. This gives us hope not just for the next life but for today—the today of
dirty laundry, broken promises, unmet expectations, and ongoing tension. The hope
for full redemption must be so present in our everyday reality that we can live with
peace, courage, and joy, especially when we are surviving a season we didn't expect.

NOT WHAT I SIGNED UP FOR, PAGES 192–193

We end our time where we began: reflecting on what a life of resilient faith looks like through the person of Joseph. Through the tests and trials, Joseph developed a mature, resilient trust in God that allowed him to say with certainty, "You meant evil against me, but God meant it for good" (Genesis 50:20, NASB). If we allow God to shape all of our seasons—the ones we choose and the ones we never invited—we will develop into people of both deep trust and resilient faith.

MAIN POINT

Resilient faith develops in our unexpected seasons.

RECAP

Look over last week's homework. **Share any of your reflections from what you learned during your daily studies or while reading *Not What I Signed Up For*.**

Tune in to video session 6: "The Story of Sovereignty"

 **VIDEO NOTES**

1. The process of redemption impacts everyone it touches.

2. Jesus came to "reconcile to himself all things" (Colossians 1:20)—and that includes you!

3. Revival is real, experienced in the fullness of heaven and in glimpses throughout our lives.

4. Joseph's story—as well as yours and mine—is embedded in the great big story of God's redeeming love.

OPENING GROUP CONVERSATION

1. Do you have any favorite hand-me-down or "recycled" items in your home? What do you like about them? What is the story behind one of them?

2. Who have been the primary influences in your faith journey? Has your own understanding of redemption been impacted by someone else's redemption story?

3. If you were to describe someone as "a person of resilient faith," what qualities do you think they would have?

TO THE WORD TOGETHER

Let's read the end of the Joseph story in Genesis:

> Now that their father was dead, Joseph's brothers became fearful. "Now Joseph will show his anger and pay us back for all the wrong we did to him," they said.

So they sent this message to Joseph: "Before your father died, he instructed us to say to you: 'Please forgive your brothers for the great wrong they did to you—for their sin in treating you so cruelly.' So we, the servants of the God of your father, beg you to forgive our sin." When Joseph received the message, he broke down and wept. Then his brothers came and threw themselves down before Joseph. "Look, we are your slaves!" they said.

But Joseph replied, "Don't be afraid of me. Am I God, that I can punish you? You intended to harm me, but God intended it all for good. He brought me to this position so I could save the lives of many people. No, don't be afraid. I will continue to take care of you and your children." So he reassured them by speaking kindly to them.

So Joseph and his brothers and their families continued to live in Egypt. Joseph lived to the age of 110. He lived to see three generations of descendants of his son Ephraim, and he lived to see the birth of the children of Manasseh's son Makir, whom he claimed as his own.

GENESIS 50:15-23, NLT

1. How did the brothers react to their father's death? What emotions do you think they were experiencing?

2. What do you believe caused Joseph to weep?

3. Joseph's story speaks to God's provision even in affliction. **Imagine if you were in Joseph's place. What part of his life stands out to you as the one in which you would have experienced God's goodness? (Use your imagination!)**

This week, we are going to explore how Joseph's righteous life is a shadow of the life of Christ, our ultimate example of humility, holiness, and love. Let's read the following passage from Hebrews 9 together. For context, Jesus is being compared to the priestly system set up by Moses after the Israelites were led out of Egypt—the very story that starts when Joseph moved his family there! In this system, the priests were set apart from the people to offer sacrifices for their sins—a practice that had to be repeated over and over again. **Let's look at how that system changed because of Christ:**

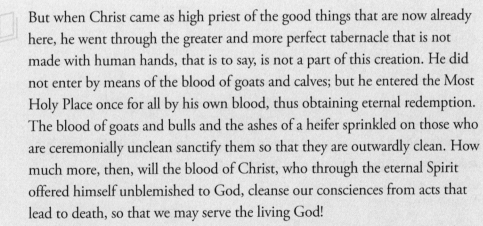

But when Christ came as high priest of the good things that are now already here, he went through the greater and more perfect tabernacle that is not made with human hands, that is to say, is not a part of this creation. He did not enter by means of the blood of goats and calves; but he entered the Most Holy Place once for all by his own blood, thus obtaining eternal redemption. The blood of goats and bulls and the ashes of a heifer sprinkled on those who are ceremonially unclean sanctify them so that they are outwardly clean. How much more, then, will the blood of Christ, who through the eternal Spirit offered himself unblemished to God, cleanse our consciences from acts that lead to death, so that we may serve the living God!

For this reason Christ is the mediator of a new covenant, that those who are called may receive the promised eternal inheritance—now that he has died as a ransom to set them free from the sins committed under the first covenant.

HEBREWS 9:11-15

4. How did Christ obtain eternal redemption for us?

5. What two things does the blood of Christ do for us?

6. What is the "promised eternal inheritance"? (To find the answer, you may want to skim through Hebrews 4:14-16; 7:24-28; 12:28.)

7. Now think about how these promises of God connect from Joseph's story into Jesus' story and then into our own lives:

💡 APPLICATION

1. We started our study with three important promises drawn from Genesis 50:19-20: Do not be afraid; God is here; God has plans to accomplish good for you and through you. **With the full story of Joseph fresh in your mind, how do you interpret these promises for your own life? How does knowing Jesus affect the way you understand these promises?**

2. How would you describe the character of Joseph? What events in your story have shaped your character in similar ways? In what ways would you like to grow more like Joseph?

👤 YOUR ONE THING

As the group closes, take two minutes to record one key takeaway from this session.

What words or ideas do you want to hang on to as you go into this week?

A CLOSING PRAYER

God, give us faith to believe You're at work in our stories.
God, give us faith to believe Your intentions are good.
God, give us faith to believe . . . You.

We ask for the joy that comes from Your presence,
the confidence that comes from Your acceptance,
the healing that comes with Your mercy,

and the great blessing of Your love.

Grant us the humility to serve others like You do
and the trust to believe that Your mercy covers our weaknesses
and that Your powerful grace overcomes our failings. Amen.

ON YOUR OWN
DAILY STUDY

SESSION 6

THE JOSEPH BLESSING

This week we are going to review our own progress as we look at our lives through the story of Joseph and, ultimately, the redeeming work of Christ. Even if the circumstances of your life are the same today as when you started this study, my prayer is that your heart would be in a different place—more open to God's comfort, more aware of God's presence, and more trusting of God's goodness, even in difficulties.

 ## REFLECT

Begin by reading the passage below.

Joseph said to them, "Don't be afraid. Am I in the place of God? You intended to harm me, but God intended it for good to accomplish what is now being done, the saving of many lives."
GENESIS 50:19-20

Repeat this inventory you took in session 1:

1. Joseph makes this statement at the end of his ordeal when he can look back and clearly see God at work. It can be challenging to have this perspective when you're in the middle of a trying season. **When your circumstances are difficult, which of the following descriptions are most true of you? Circle all that apply or adjust the statement(s) to be accurate for you.**

    a. I find myself anxious about the future.

    b. I second-guess my decisions and blame my past choices for this pain.

    c. I often find myself blaming others or my circumstances for my pain.

d. I feel like I'm being punished.

e. I have a hard time trusting God's intentions and wonder if He has forgotten about me.

f. I feel angry about what's happened.

g. I feel resigned that nothing can change.

2. What promises can you refer back to that will help you continue to trust in God, even in unexpected seasons? Aim to record three to five verses below that you want to keep close to your heart. (You can use the concordance in your Bible to find verses or choose some from the list that begins on page 205).

In session 1, we learned:

This is the heart of the matter—when we turn toward Christ in uncertainty, we experience the deepest growth in our faith.

3. How have you grown in your faith over these last weeks? What have you learned about God? What have you learned about yourself?

CLOSING MEDITATION

Read the following verses:

> Even youths grow tired and weary,
>   and young men stumble and fall;
> but those who hope in the LORD
>   will renew their strength.
> They will soar on wings like eagles;
>   they will run and not grow weary,
>   they will walk and not be faint.

ISAIAH 40:30-31

Take a few moments to rest in God's presence and let Him fill you with His strength. You may want to use the following breath prayer to focus your attention:

(Inhale) Lord, as I hope in You,
(Exhale) You renew my strength.

As you reflect on these words, let any cares or concerns rise up in your mind. Then imagine leaving them in God's loving care. Try to spend at least five minutes in this space of focused rest with God.

THE PROMISES HE KEEPS

 READ

Chapter 11, *Not What I Signed Up For*

Use this space to capture any key phrases or takeaways from the chapter that you want to remember:

Today take a few minutes to begin intentionally listening to your own redemption and revival story—the one God is writing in your life. **To start, center your attention on this truth from session 2:**

A foundation of faith will not fail even when all else does.

In order to be real and redeemed people, we have to be able to hold together the reality of our loss with the hope of redemption.

REFLECT

Let's revisit the following question from day 2 of session 2:

1. When you think through your own experiences with loss, how would you characterize your relationship with God in the midst of it? Check any/all that apply.

   ☐ I don't know what to do with my sadness, so I skip it and stuff it.

   ☐ I feel angry and confused about why some things have happened and tend to dwell on it.

   ☐ I've tried to process these losses, but I feel stuck.

   ☐ I realize that God has been close to me and that my faith has grown through loss.

   ☐ Other:_____.

In Jesus' great teaching, the Sermon on the Mount, He talks about those who are truly blessed. For example, He says, "Blessed are those who mourn, for they will be comforted" (Matthew 5:4).

2. How have you experienced God's comfort during unexpected seasons? What are some of the ways you've seen God show up to care for you?

CLOSING MEDITATION

Read the following verses from the Sermon on the Mount:

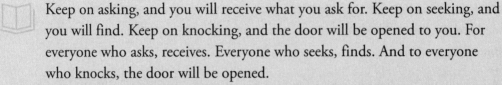

Keep on asking, and you will receive what you ask for. Keep on seeking, and you will find. Keep on knocking, and the door will be opened to you. For everyone who asks, receives. Everyone who seeks, finds. And to everyone who knocks, the door will be opened.

You parents—if your children ask for a loaf of bread, do you give them a stone instead? Or if they ask for a fish, do you give them a snake? Of course not! So if you sinful people know how to give good gifts to your children, how much more will your heavenly Father give good gifts to those who ask him.

MATTHEW 7:7-11, NLT

Take a few moments to rest in God's presence and let Him speak to your heart. You may want to use a breath prayer to focus your attention, inhaling and exhaling these words:

(Inhale) Heavenly Father,

(Exhale) You give good gifts.

Ask God to reveal to you the good gifts He's given to you in this season. Try not to rush ahead and answer for Him. Simply rest in His presence, expecting Him to show up.

Record any of the gifts God reveals to you here:

THE TESTS OF YOUR CHARACTER

In session 3, we focused on how tests of our character produce humility. We discovered that the rigorous journey through an unexpected season is an invitation to a rooted, deep, and lively trust in God.

 ## REFLECT

Consider how you've grown in humility over these past weeks by reviewing the same prompt from session 3:

1. How would you describe your relationship with humility? Circle one or more of the letters below.

   a. I struggle with humility when it comes to not overcontrolling my life and relationships.
   b. I struggle with humility when it comes to admitting I need help.
   c. I struggle with humility when it comes to respecting and caring about people even after they've hurt me or someone I love.
   d. Other: _____.

2. As you reflect on Joseph's story, summarize what it looks like to show up with humility, no matter the circumstance. (For reference, check out how Joseph behaved with Potiphar's wife, while he was in prison, or when he was with his brothers.)

3. **Now turn once again to Jesus' words from the Sermon on the Mount:**

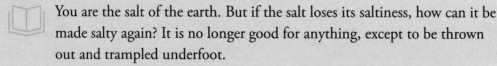

You are the salt of the earth. But if the salt loses its saltiness, how can it be made salty again? It is no longer good for anything, except to be thrown out and trampled underfoot.

You are the light of the world. A town built on a hill cannot be hidden. Neither do people light a lamp and put it under a bowl. Instead they put it on its stand, and it gives light to everyone in the house. In the same way, let your light shine before others, that they may see your good deeds and glorify your Father in heaven.

MATTHEW 5:13-16

Jesus uses salt and light as a metaphor to describe how we are to engage with the world. A little salt gives food more flavor. Light can guide the way, change our vision, and even bring healing. I've heard a friend say, "A little salt makes everything better. . . . As Christians, we should enter the world the same way. What if our goal was to make every room a little better because we were there?"

a. **What would it look like to show up in a way that makes everything better? List the people with whom you'll interact over the next eight to twelve hours and consider how you could improve their days:**

 CLOSING MEDITATION

Let's devote the rest of our time to the good work of asking God to bless those we will come into contact with today. **For guidance, read this verse from Acts 20, a perfect picture of humility in life and confidence in grace:**

However, I consider my life worth nothing to me; my only aim is to finish the race and complete the task the Lord Jesus has given me—the task of testifying to the good news of God's grace.

ACTS 20:24

Take a moment to bring to mind each person you'll interact with today, committing to the work of being salt and light to them.

Pray your own requests, or use this breath prayer:

(Inhale) Father, I bring _____ to You today.

(Exhale) May they know Your grace,

(Inhale) experience Your blessing,

(Exhale) and feel Your love.

When we pray for those we relate with, God increases our awareness of their needs as well as our compassion for them. Choosing to pray a blessing over someone is a great act of humility, especially if your relationship is difficult. As you pray for them, don't be surprised if, bit by bit, your heart begins to soften and change toward the person. God has not called us to freedom for our own sakes only, but for the sake of blessing others with that grace.

May that be true, in increasing measure, for each person you are blessed to serve today!

OUR TRANSFORMING IDENTITY

 READ

Chapter 12, *Not What I Signed Up For*

Use this space to capture any key phrases or takeaways from the chapter that you want to remember:

Today we wrap up our reading with the greatest news of all: our transformed identity in Christ. In session 4, we focused on this truth:

> *One of our deepest expressions of faith is trusting God enough to continue moving forward, even in circumstances we don't understand.*

REFLECT

Over the last several weeks, we've been working to raise our awareness of God's presence in our lives. Here's the related prompt again from session 4:

1. What's your current awareness of God during a normal day?

   ☐ I almost always pray or talk to God throughout the day and experience Christ through daily spiritual practices.

   ☐ If I'm struggling or stressed, I usually remember to pray and ask for help.

   ☐ I generally don't think to have conversations with God, especially when I'm busy.

   ☐ I try to get to church and Bible study, and that's the extent of it for me.

2. How has your awareness of God's daily presence grown over these past weeks? Where have you seen this change?

3. When you feel connected to God, how do you show up in difficult circumstances?

4. How has God answered your prayers during this study? Look back over your homework to refresh your memory on what you've brought to God. Some areas where you might be experiencing God in your life include:

   ☐ Bearing the fruit of the Spirit (see Galatians 5:22-23)

   ☐ Growing in love for your enemies

☐ Releasing bitterness or unforgiveness

☐ Developing discernment toward someone or something that could only come from God (see Colossians 2:2-3)

☐ Gaining a different perspective on your previous or current difficulties

☐ Other:_____

Friend, I believe that by simply showing up for God, faithfully seeking His Word, and resting in His presence, you will see Him doing a great work in your heart. You may feel big changes or small, incremental steps of healing. But regardless of where you find yourself today, God is not done with you. He continues to pour out His healing love, revival power, and redeeming grace in every inch of your life. As you close your time with Him today, praise Him for His continued love and mercy toward you!

CLOSING MEDITATION

This is a great opportunity to write your own breath prayer of praise. I'll include a few verses to draw from. **Simply put two phrases together that form your prayer of praise, and then give yourself five minutes to worship in Jesus' presence, bringing Him your pure love and gratitude.**

Verses of praise

Who is like You among the gods, Lord?
Who is like You, majestic in holiness,
Awesome in praises, working wonders?
EXODUS 15:11, NASB

I will be glad and rejoice in you;
    I will sing the praises of your name,
        O Most High.
PSALM 9:2

You did it: you changed wild lament
    into whirling dance;
You ripped off my black mourning band
    and decked me with wildflowers.
I'm about to burst with song;
    I can't keep quiet about you.
GOD, my God,
    I can't thank you enough.

PSALM 30:11-12, MSG

I will rejoice greatly in the LORD,
My soul will be joyful in my God;
For He has clothed me with garments of salvation,
He has wrapped me with a robe of righteousness.

ISAIAH 61:10, NASB

Amen!
Praise and glory
and wisdom and thanks and honor
and power and strength
be to our God for ever and ever.
Amen!

REVELATION 7:12

Your breath prayer:

READ

Conclusion, *Not What I Signed Up For*

What would it be like to come out of your unexpected season believing in *more* for your life? Not more prosperity in the form of luxury goods, vacations, or promotions—I think if we've made it this far, we know blessing is not about *that.* But what if you believed in a spiritual prosperity that allowed you to thrive regardless of the season you found yourself in? What if you had a crystal clear vision of the kind of dream you could believe in, a dream in which you experienced more of God's goodness and love each day? The ancient philosopher Aristotle once described such an expectation this way: "Hope is a waking dream."

The apostle Paul lays it out even more clearly: "Praise be to the God and Father of our Lord Jesus Christ, who has blessed us in the heavenly realms with every spiritual blessing in Christ" (Ephesians 1:3). You and I offer praise to our God and Father because we have every spiritual blessing. During this study, you have learned that blessing is something that happens to you and through you; however, do you know what a spiritual blessing is? **Let's review what these look like and then make it personal together as our closing act of praise.**

REFLECT

Read the following verses, and underline the blessing in each one:

> When God created mankind, he made them in the likeness of God.
> He created them male and female and blessed them.
> **GENESIS 5:1-2**

The LORD gives strength to his people;
> the LORD blesses his people with
>> peace.

PSALM 29:11

Taste and see that the LORD is good;
> blessed is the one who takes refuge
>> in him.

PSALM 34:8

Blessed is the one you discipline,
> LORD,
> the one you teach from your law.

PSALM 94:12

Whoever gives heed to instruction prospers,
> and blessed is the one who trusts in the
>> LORD.

PROVERBS 16:20

Christ will make his home in your hearts as you trust
in him. Your roots will grow down into God's love and
keep you strong.

EPHESIANS 3:17, NLT

May you be strengthened with all power,
according to [God's] glorious might.

COLOSSIANS 1:11, HCSB

May the Lord make your love for one another and
for all people grow and overflow.

1 THESSALONIANS 3:12, NLT

Now, look back over what you've underlined and write out a blessing manifesto! Change the blessing to make it personal for your life. I've completed the first two for you:

I am made in God's image and blessed for simply being created.

I am blessed with peace.

These are the blessings you are promised in Christ! You can claim these as your own. You can expect God to show up this way in your life. No matter how deep your pain or how unexpected the season, victory is yours because of what Christ has done for you. He has a plan. If you are seeking to follow Him, you are right where you need to be for Him to bless you with every spiritual blessing in Christ.

> The way of the Cross was always the plan. Only a great love for a precious possession is worth great cost. And through Christ, God declared that we are His great love, His precious possession. This is the story that begins in Genesis and continues today: Our great and loving God extends His heart of mercy, love, and belonging, over and over again. Our great God covers our sin, redeems our past, and frees us to live out our future.
>
> *NOT WHAT I SIGNED UP FOR*, PAGE 215

⊙ CLOSING MEDITATION

I'd love to invite you to end your time in this study with a deep sense of God's delight in your faithfulness and His affection for who you really are—no masks, no pretense, no performing. Unexpected seasons strip away all those facades, and we are left with just ourselves. And in this very place God shows us that He has loved us all along, just as we are.

Can I leave you with a blessing?

May God call you by name,
rejoice over you with singing,
clothe you in His righteousness,
crown you with His love,
fill you with His grace,
and direct your every step.
Amen!

A Note for Leaders

If you are stepping into the role of group leader with some trepidation, I have some news for you: No one feels ready to be a leader.[1]

If you are new to facilitating a group, or if you are terrified to lead a group of your peers, rest assured that you are not alone! Everyone is intimidated when they first lead a group. So here's some good news for you about leadership: You don't need to have the most Bible knowledge or be the most patient or experienced person in the room. You simply need to be available and willing—available to show up for your group and willing to grow through the process.

A great group leader doesn't need to have all the answers (in fact, if someone thinks they know every answer, that is usually a sign that the person is *not* a great leader). The best group leaders do two things. First, they make the group *safe*. They start and end meetings on time, keep the group on track with questions, and gently redirect if one group member is trying to give advice or "fix" someone else. Second, these leaders make the group *honest*. They are willing to be vulnerable when responding to questions, create space for people to share fully and openly, and encourage each member of the group to grow.

A group that provides both safety and honesty is a setting in which powerful development can happen.

Here are some other helpful hints as you lead your group:

- This study works equally well in a ministry setting, such as a larger group situated around tables, or in a home or small group setting.
- As the leader, you set the tone for the depth and authenticity of your group. Your job is not to have all the answers but to be open so that people can bring their questions with vulnerability and feel heard and understood. You do that by sharing from your own life and by giving others the space to share.
- You also set the tone through your own preparation. By previewing the video and working through the questions in the guide in advance, you'll have a better sense of what questions to focus on and how the group is likely to go each time you meet. Your preparation also tells your group that you value their time and expect this experience to be important and meaningful. The tone of the leader determines the tone of the group.
- Communication as a leader is key. Make sure you connect with your group between sessions via email, text, etc., to clarify what the group should do to prepare for the next meeting and to remind them when and where you'll be meeting.
- Your group will most likely not have time to respond to every question during your time together—and that's okay! Instead, try to hit at least one of the questions from each section every time you meet, but focus on what's best for the group.

My prayer is that you experience surprising refreshment in the Lord as you serve so that you can refresh others. I pray that God will bless you with wisdom and compassion for the people in the group—and perhaps in new ways for yourself. And "I pray that you, being rooted and established in love, may have power, together with all the Lord's holy people, to grasp how wide and long and high and deep is the love of Christ" (Ephesians 3:17-18). Amen!

WEEKLY LEADER'S GUIDE

The following guidelines are meant to help you manage your time and get the most out of your group sessions. Remember, these instructions are intended to give you confidence as you get to know your group members and respond to what works best for them. It's said that 90 percent of leadership is just showing up, so show up for your group—be fully present, be fully yourself, and pray that God will use your faithfulness to bring Him glory. It's a prayer He loves to answer.

Welcome (10 minutes)

At the first meeting, make sure everyone knows one another's names. Go over the basics: stage of life, workplace, what drew the person to the group. Don't forget to share what prompted you to start or lead the group! (Note: For session 1 only, I suggest planning for a slightly extended welcome time to allow for group introductions.)

Recap (10 minutes)

In this study, we've made time for the group to share some insights and questions from the previous week's homework—which will help you know what direction you might want to take the rest of your group time each week. It's also an opportunity for members to get better acquainted.

Even if your group members know each other well, connection time is a chance each week to find out something new, to hear something different, and to allow space for old friends to surprise one another with new details! If your group members don't know one another well or at all, this time is *crucial* because it gives everyone a chance to be themselves without jumping right into a conversation that might be intimidating to someone with less Bible study experience.

Video Time (10 minutes)

Tune in to the session. Make sure everyone knows they can take notes in their guide as they listen.

Opening Group Conversation (10 minutes)

You may not be able to answer every question in the time you have, so pick one or two to focus on and then return to other questions in this section if you have extra time.

To the Word Together (20–30 minutes)

This section is designed to help everyone get comfortable exploring the Bible as a group. It can be helpful to have an extra Bible handy so you can pass it around and read some passages aloud.

Application (15 minutes)

This is where participants will discover the takeaway—where it gets real. Application can be tricky at first, as groups gauge how comfortable they are with being vulnerable with one another. Be sure to leave enough silence to allow people to speak—which usually is long enough to feel *slightly* awkward!

Your One Thing (5 minutes)

Each week, we've made space for everyone to take a minute or two to write the one point they want to remember from either the previous week's homework or that day's lesson. This gives you the opportunity to invite participants to go around the circle and simply read what they've written—an easy way to get everyone to participate and reflect on what they've been learning.

Prayer (5 minutes)

In the first session, it's best for you to be the one to close in prayer. As you get to know your group, you can move to sharing prayer requests and then praying together. Be mindful of those in your group who are exploring faith or are new believers. Avoid "Christianese"—the tendency for Christians to use terms that those new to the faith don't understand. Pray sincerely and simply, and you'll help others learn to approach God in the same way.

Don't forget to close your time by covering the basics—when and where you'll meet next, an encouragement to complete the homework and assigned readings from the book (which are embedded within the homework), and any other logistical details.

Simple communication and follow-up will help each person in your group feel known and cared for, which goes a *long* way!

USING THE STUDY FOR EIGHT WEEKS

Some groups will prefer to stretch the study into an eight-session experience. If you choose to do so with your group, you can devote the first session to simply getting to know one another, distributing materials, and setting expectations. You can then use sessions 2 through 6 as written. I'd encourage you to meet over a meal for the final session, inviting each person to prepare a verbal or written "gift" for each member of the group. These could be centered around a prompt like "What I've learned from you . . . ," or "What I appreciate about you . . . ," or "You've encouraged my faith by . . ." Sharing these reflections can be an incredibly meaningful way to celebrate the growth you've experienced together.

PROMISES OF GOD

HIS GOODNESS

Give thanks to the LORD, for he is good; his love endures forever.

1 CHRONICLES 16:34

Taste and see that the LORD is good; blessed is the one who takes refuge in him.

PSALM 34:8

For the LORD is good and his love endures forever; his faithfulness continues through all generations.

PSALM 100:5

The LORD is good to all; he has compassion on all he has made.

PSALM 145:9

He gives strength to the weary and increases the power of the weak.

ISAIAH 40:29

Those who hope in the LORD will renew their strength. They will soar on wings like eagles; they will run and not grow weary, they will walk and not be faint.

ISAIAH 40:31

The LORD is good, a refuge in times of trouble. He cares for those who trust in him.

NAHUM 1:7

Every good and perfect gift is from above, coming down from the Father of the heavenly lights, who does not change like shifting shadows.

JAMES 1:17

HIS PRESENCE

The LORD himself goes before you and will be with you; he will never leave you nor forsake you. Do not be afraid; do not be discouraged.

DEUTERONOMY 31:8

Where can I go from your Spirit? Where can I flee from your presence? If I go up to the heavens, you are there; if I make my bed in the depths, you are there. If I rise on the wings of the dawn, if I settle on the far side of the sea, even there your hand will guide me, your right hand will hold me fast.

PSALM 139:7-10

When you pass through the waters, I will be with you; and when you pass through the rivers, they will not sweep over you. When you walk through the fire, you will not be burned; the flames will not set you ablaze.

ISAIAH 43:2

Teach these new disciples to obey all the commands I have given you. And be sure of this: I am with you always, even to the end of the age.

MATTHEW 28:20, NLT

HIS BLESSING

The lions may grow weak and hungry, but those who seek the LORD lack no good thing.

PSALM 34:10

"For I know the plans I have for you," declares the LORD, "plans to prosper you and not to harm you, plans to give you hope and a future."

JEREMIAH 29:11

Do not let your hearts be troubled. You believe in God; believe also in me. My Father's house has many rooms; if that were not so, would I have told you that I am going there to prepare a place for you? And if I go and prepare a place for you, I will come back and take you to be with me that you also may be where I am.

JOHN 14:1-3

Peace I leave with you; my peace I give you. I do not give to you as the world gives. Do not let your hearts be troubled and do not be afraid.

JOHN 14:27

Yes, I am the vine; you are the branches. Those who remain in me, and I in them, will produce much fruit. For apart from me you can do nothing.

JOHN 15:5, NLT

He who did not spare his own Son, but gave him up for us all—how will he not also, along with him, graciously give us all things?

ROMANS 8:32

God is able to bless you abundantly, so that in all things at all times, having all that you need, you will abound in every good work.

2 CORINTHIANS 9:8

Do not be anxious about anything, but in every situation, by prayer and petition, with thanksgiving, present your requests to God. And the peace of God, which transcends all understanding, will guard your hearts and your minds in Christ Jesus.

PHILIPPIANS 4:6-7

THE ASSURANCE OF OUR SALVATION

If my people, who are called by my name, will humble themselves and pray and seek my face and turn from their wicked ways, then I will hear from heaven, and I will forgive their sin and will heal their land.

2 CHRONICLES 7:14

For God so loved the world that he gave his one and only Son, that whoever believes in him shall not perish but have eternal life.

JOHN 3:16

If the Son sets you free, you will be free indeed.

JOHN 8:36

If you declare with your mouth, "Jesus is Lord," and believe in your heart that God raised him from the dead, you will be saved. For it is with your heart that you believe and are justified, and it is with your mouth that you profess your faith and are saved.

ROMANS 10:9-10

If we confess our sins, he is faithful and just and will forgive us our sins and purify us from all unrighteousness.

1 JOHN 1:9

Notes

FIRST THINGS FIRST: A WORD TO READERS

1. Parker Palmer, *A Hidden Wholeness: The Journey toward an Undivided Life* (San Francisco, CA: Jossey-Bass, 2004), 58–59.

SESSION 1: THE JOSEPH BLESSING

1. Megan Brooks, "Americans' Biggest Source of Anxiety? Hint: It's Not COVID," Medscape, July 14, 2022, https://www.medscape.com/viewarticle/977188?reg=1#vp_1.
2. If you are one of the many with an anxiety disorder, simply "trusting God" is not the answer to this complicated illness. If your anxiety interferes with your ability to lead a normal life, I encourage you to seek out treatment, which can help you address your worry alongside your spiritual practices.
3. *Merriam-Webster Online Dictionary*, s.v. "praise," accessed June 2, 2023, https://www.merriam-webster.com/dictionary/praise.
4. Bible Study Tools, s.v. "glory," accessed June 2, 2023, https://www.biblestudytools.com/dictionary/glory/.

SESSION 2: THE PROMISES HE KEEPS

1. Based on *Merriam-Webster Online Dictionary*, s.v. "bless," accessed June 2, 2023, https://www.merriam-webster.com/dictionary/bless.
2. Sarah Epstein, "4 Types of Grief No One Told You About," *Psychology Today*, April 17, 2019, https://www.psychologytoday.com/us/blog/between-the-generations/201904/4-types-grief-no-one-told-you-about.
3. Spiros Zodhiates, ed., *Hebrew-Greek Key Word Study Bible: New International Version* (Chattanooga, TN: AMG Publishers, 1996), s.v. "bahan," 1506.

SESSION 3: THE TESTS OF YOUR CHARACTER

1. Thomas Merton, *No Man Is an Island* (Boston: Shambhala Publications, 2005), 119.
2. Proverbs 11:2, ESV.
3. John Ortberg, *When the Game Is Over, It All Goes Back in the Box* (Grand Rapids, MI: Zondervan, 2007), 149.
4. See note on 1 Corinthians 1:18, *ESV Study Bible* (Wheaton, IL: Crossway, 2008).

SESSION 4: THE WORK OF PATIENCE

1. Archdiocese of Saint Paul and Minneapolis, "St. Francis of Assisi: Make Me an Instrument of Your Peace," accessed June 6, 2023, https://www.archspm.org/faith-and-discipleship/prayer/catholic-prayers/st-francis-of-assisi-make-me-an-instrument-of-your-peace/.
2. This quote is often attributed to Sir Winston Churchill, but its origin hasn't been verified. See Richard M. Langworth, "Churchill on the Optimist and Pessimist," June 20, 2017, https://richardlangworth.com/optimist-pessimists.
3. Mark Vroegop, "The 4 Basics of Lament," Crossway website, July 14, 2020, https://www.crossway.org/articles/the-4-basics-of-lament/.

SESSION 5: THE POWER OF REDEMPTION

1. Spiros Zodhiates, ed., *Hebrew-Greek Key Word Study Bible: New International Version* (Chattanooga, TN: AMG Publishers, 1996), s.v. *"metanoeo,"* 1651.
2. Zodhiates, *Hebrew-Greek Key Word Study Bible,* s.v. *"dikaioo,"* 1608.

A NOTE FOR LEADERS

1. As a Bible teacher, I've coached many small group leaders as they got started. I first offered the following guidelines and suggestions in *The Struggle Is Real Participant's Guide* (Carol Stream, IL: Tyndale, 2018).

About the Author

Nicole Unice is a pastor and leadership coach who facilitates environments of safety and vulnerability so that leaders and teams can courageously identify obstacles keeping them from their maximum potential. As a sought-after speaker, Nicole has a down-to-earth style that allows even the largest gathering to feel conversational. Nicole is the author of several books focused on spiritual transformation and is a featured speaker through RightNow Media and Punchline. She holds degrees from the College of William and Mary and from Gordon-Conwell Theological Seminary. Nicole and her husband, Dave, live in Richmond, Virginia, with their three children and two pups. Visit her online at nicoleunice.com.

rightnow MEDIA

FREE BIBLE STUDY VIDEOS FOR

NOT WHAT I
SIGNED UP FOR

Because you have purchased *Not What I Signed Up For*, you also have free access to the companion Bible study videos—perfect for group study or personal devotions.

Scan this code to access these videos for free!

CP1955

Have you ever found yourself in an unexpected season, thinking (and saying to God), *This is not what I signed up for*? Join popular Bible teacher Nicole Unice, who helps you see how God uses life's hard times, twists, turns, and in-between spaces to grow something essential in your soul.

Not What I Signed Up For:
This book provides accessible tools to help you navigate the unexpected and disorienting seasons of life with strength, hope, and perspective. Drawing from the biblical story of Joseph, Nicole demonstrates how you can move through trial and temptation to trust.

*Not What I Signed Up For Study Guide:
This is a six-session workbook companion to the *Not What I Signed Up For* book. It's a great resource for church groups, Bible studies, and anyone who desires to navigate life's unexpected and chaotic seasons in order to find renewed hope and purpose.

It's time to transform your relationships
at home, in love, and at work.
Are you ready for your miracle moment?

The Miracle Moment Discover the moment in every conversation that can change the whole relationship. Popular speaker Nicole Unice helps you discover the practical tools, words, and boundaries that will transform conflict into connection—even when you're tempted to shut up, blow up, or give up.

The Miracle Moment Participant's Guide A six-session workbook created for group or individual use. Accompanying DVD available for purchase. Streaming videos provided online at rightnowmedia.org.

Visit Nicole online at nicoleunice.com.

CP1686

BOOKS AND MORE BY NICOLE UNICE

She's Got Issues

Brave Enough

The Struggle Is Real

DVDs and streaming videos also available.

Available wherever books are sold. TYNDALE.COM